Walk You To WEALTH

By

Kevin C. Feig, CFP,® CPA/PFS

1

TABLE OF CONTENTS

PART ONE: WHO AM I?

"Give up being perfect for being authentic."

Hal Elrod

I have two children, and when they were 6 and 4, we started participating in one of our town's Halloween traditions known as "ghosting." This normally involves driving your son or daughter to their friends' houses at night so that they can run out of the car, drop a bag of candy at the front door, ring the bell and then run back to the car without being seen and disappear like a ghost. The key word in the last sentence is "normally." My family does it a little differently. My two boys like me to ghost with them. So yes, this is exactly what you are thinking it is. Imagine for a second that it's late at night, dark outside, and there is a grown man creeping through your front yard, hiding behind your bushes, and peering through the windows of your home where you have a small child inside!

One year, during our last "ghosting" of the night, we arrived at my oldest son's friend's house, whom I had nicknamed Johnny Rockets because he had so much energy. Unbeknownst to me, Johnny Rockets liked to try to catch 'ghosters' and would wait and hide himself. So, we sneak to the front door, carefully avoiding the security lights over the garage, drop the candy, ring the bell, and then run. A half-second later, the front door flew open, and Johnny Rockets leapt out in his pajamas, carrying a flashlight, and proceeded to chase us barefoot down the road shouting, "Stop, I caught you!" At this point, I am a grown man running down a dark street to a parked car with no lights on, while being chased by a small child who is screaming, "Stop, I caught you!" Fortunately, no one called the police, and we had a good laugh when Johnny Rockets caught us by the car. So, what does any of this have to do with personal finance? Everything! I want you to know who I am as a person before we start talking about a single dollar. I'm a husband and a father who will do almost anything to have a laugh with my two boys! I also want you to know why I wrote this book before we take our first step together, but let's start with a bit more on the "who" before we move on to the "why."

I grew up in a middle-class family in Queens, NY. For those who have never been to Queens, it's a densely populated and diverse suburb of Manhattan (think Spiderman without the superpowers). My dad was a sanitation worker, or as he would say a "garbage man," and he also owned an Irish pub. The pub was originally owned by my maternal grandfather who started it when he and my grandmother emigrated from Ireland. This is the American dream in about two sentences. My mom, whom I called Mims, stayed at home for most of my childhood, raising me and my two older brothers, and later, she worked as an administrator for a hospital.

My parents were amazing, which is a wild understatement. My dad worked for both the sanitation and managing the pub for the better part of my childhood. I fondly remember going to the pub on the occasional Sunday morning to help him clean, which mostly meant hanging out with my dad and walking to the convenience store to buy some candy for me and a coffee for him. Mims, on the other hand, was the life of any party. During a family trip to Las Vegas to celebrate my 21st birthday, I still remember my now wife not noticing a man casually walking down Fremont Street on a pair of stilts, because she was too distracted by my mom who was dancing up and down the street. I'm not sure what the formal definition is of "life of the party," but I feel confident that it should include the ability to take attention away from a man walking down the street on stilts!

As far as I was concerned, we were rich, and my parents always paid for everything with cash. For the younger audience, cash was something we used before we tapped cell phones to pay for everything. I remember staying at a hotel for a family wedding where Mims tried, but failed, to convince the front desk clerk to accept $1,000 of cash for our four hotel rooms!

I had a great childhood and learned so much about life from my parents. I was also fortunate to attend great schools; however, despite my incredible parents and great education, like most kids, I never learned about money, investing, or personal finance. This is no criticism of my parents, as they couldn't have taught me what they themselves never learned. It also wasn't, and much to my horror, still isn't, a subject taught at most schools.

As a young adult, I attended Fairfield University where I earned a Bachelor of Science in Accounting in 2002 and a Master's in Business Administration in 2003.

My first job after graduation was at a large accounting firm, where I was responsible for reviewing the financial statements of companies like Pepsi and Domino Sugar. These companies made tangible products that I could see, taste, feel, and smell (on a side note, nothing smells surprisingly worse than a sugar factory). As I started to explore new opportunities, I interviewed at one of the largest financial institutions in the country, during which I said, "I know nothing about financial services," to which the interviewer replied, "That's probably not something you want to say in an interview here," but it was the truth. After working with companies that made simple products like soda and sugar, financial services seemed like the exact opposite. It was abstract and confusing. It felt like an elaborate magic trick that you couldn't quite figure out unless you were on the inside. Despite my honest answers during the interview, I received a job offer and worked in risk management for approximately 15 years until I had the opportunity to join a cryptocurrency exchange.

Along my journey, I've become a Certified Public Accountant, a Personal Financial Specialist and a CERTIFIED FINANCIAL PLANNER™. If you aren't familiar with these certifications, don't worry, it just means that I passed two difficult tests focused on accounting, and more importantly, financial planning. These paper certifications coupled with my approximately 20 years of experience in various roles in the financial services industry simply means that my approach to personal finance is at least founded in actual education and experience.

Despite my fair share of education, I'm no lawyer, but thought I should probably include the following disclaimer before you read any more of this book:

The information in this book is provided for your convenience only and is not intended to be treated as financial, investment, tax, or other advice. The information is intended to be educational and is not tailored to the investment needs of any specific individual. It is also not intended to be relied upon as a forecast and is not an offer or solicitation to buy or sell any securities or to adopt any investment strategy. The opinions expressed are those of the author. Reliance upon the guidance and information in this presentation is at the sole discretion of the individual.

You should also know that although I've had some advantages in life, such as being a white male from a loving family, I've never inherited a single dollar of my wealth.

Speaking of wealth, I'm currently on track to achieve what's known as financial independence by age 47, which simply means that I will have the "option" of working after that age. I say all of this, not from a place of boastfulness, but rather to give you some confidence that I know what I'm talking about whether you feel better about my education, professional certifications, work experience, or my personal financial achievements, which I will discuss more about in

9

the following chapters. Perhaps my qualifications or financial achievements aren't important to you, but I wouldn't want to take medical advice from someone who never completed medical school or who made terrible personal health choices, like being a smoker. If you are like me and you do care, know that I've done my homework and also practice what I preach. I am also not perfect, but I am honest to a fault. So, where I've strayed from the path or made missteps, which I will discuss, my hope is that you will learn from my mistakes and avoid those bumps in the road.

Now that we have that out of the way, and I do mean out of the way, as I've just realized that the only thing worse than talking about myself, is writing about myself, let me talk a little about why I wrote this book.

PART TWO: WHY DID I WRITE "WALK YOU TO WEALTH?"

"Wealth is the ability to fully experience life."

Henry David Thoreau

When my boys, who are 10 and 8 now, are playing with one of their neighborhood friends at my house, my wife always asks them to walk their friend home. This simple gesture was the inspiration behind the title of this book. Hopefully you've been walked home by someone in your life, whether by a date, a friend, or a parent, where the only intent is to help you get home safely. I think my two boys feel a sense of pride and responsibility in walking their friends' home, as I do on this walk with you.

The walk to wealth is much harder and more confusing than the walk home though. The business of personal finance is filled with varying advice, too many options, and terminology that makes you feel the need for a decoder ring. My goal in writing this book is to demystify, and to ultimately simplify, personal finance. I wanted to create a quick, simple, and easy-to-read guide that you could always come back to when you have questions. This book is meant to help everyone and to be as uncomplicated as possible with specific actions that you can take today to move towards a wealthier life. This book is both practical and honest, two characteristics that we don't have enough of in today's financial world. It's also not something that I ever thought I would write until recently.

During a training at my previous employer about 10 years ago, we were asked to go around the room and discuss a time in our career where we had a significant choice to make, a fork in the road, and what decision we ultimately made. The person sitting across from me worked in the accounting department and talked passionately about how he had always wanted to be an architect but chose accounting because it was a safer career. I remember feeling both sorry for him and jealous at the same time. I felt sorry that he wasn't pursuing his passion, but also envious that he knew what he wanted to do. I've never been one who knew what I wanted to be when I grew up, but I always felt that if I ever did figure it out, I would work hard to pursue it. It wasn't until my late 30s that I discovered my interest in personal finance and not until my early 40s that I realized I wanted to help people navigate this overly complicated world. It was at this time that I studied for, and passed, the Certified Financial Planning exam, which wasn't required for my role at the time and certainly isn't necessary for my job today, but it was a way for me to learn more about financial planning with the hope of one day figuring out the best way to pass on some of that knowledge.

Now that you know my "why," we should also discuss what we are walking towards. What is wealth? First, let's look at the actual definition and then I will provide my own version. According to Merriam-Webster's dictionary, wealth is defined as an "abundance of valuable material possessions or resources." I have nothing against this definition or the famed Merriam-Webster, but I think we can do better and be more specific. I love the quote we started with by Henry David Thoreau who said, "Wealth is the ability to fully experience life." Who doesn't want to fully experience life? As much as I love this quote, let's simplify it a bit more. My definition of wealth is "choice." It's that simple! The more wealth you accumulate the more choices you will have. Those choices may be small, like choosing to buy a new pair of shoes, or large, like paying for your children's college education, or donating to an important cause. It could be a bucket list trip of a lifetime or a weekend getaway with close friends. It could mean having the choice not to work, otherwise known as financial independence. Wealth to me is about choice, and although we know from the Beatles that it can't buy love, I am certain it can buy choice, which in turn can lead to lower stress, more life experiences, an increase in your sense of control, and ultimately, happiness. If I've yet to gain your trust or you don't believe me, how about a research study by Matthew Killingsworth, a senior fellow at the University of Pennsylvania's Wharton School, who found the following (a picture is worth a thousand words!):

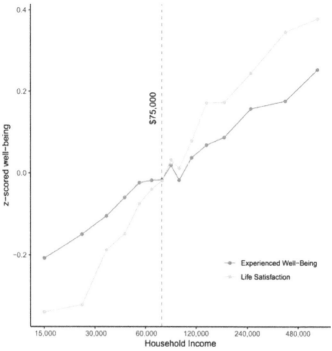

Source: Experienced well-being rises with income, even above $75,000 per year, by Matthew Killingsworth [1]

To summarize this research in a few words, wealth can buy increased well-being, satisfaction, and happiness. So, I guess, I could have named this book "Walk You To Happiness," but I'm generally not a glass half-full sort of person.

Speaking of alternative titles for this book, I also could have used a catchier title like "Overnight Millionaire," "Minutes to Millions," or anything with "Crypto" in the title, but this is not a quick fix or a get rich quick scheme. If you are looking for an overnight success plan or lots of hyperbole, there are countless Twitter "experts" you can follow, surely some sub-Reddits to join, and lots of Mad Money to watch. My point is that building wealth for most of us should be boring, even though I will try my best to make this book entertaining.

During our walk, I will discuss SIMPLE steps that we can take together towards wealth. These steps are not about perfection! As I said earlier, I am not perfect and I have made my fair share of financial mistakes, which I will discuss later, but I feel deeply passionate about simplifying saving and investing so that you can find a path to "fully experience life," a path to "choice," a path to wealth.

Are you ready to walk to wealth? Then, let's go! (If you answered "No," thanks for reading this far, and have a great rest of your day!)

PART THREE: A GLIMPSE OF THE WALK

"A journey of a thousand miles must begin with a single step."

Lao Tzu

This book details my "SIMPLE" steps to walk you to wealth, which is intended to demystify and simplify personal finance.

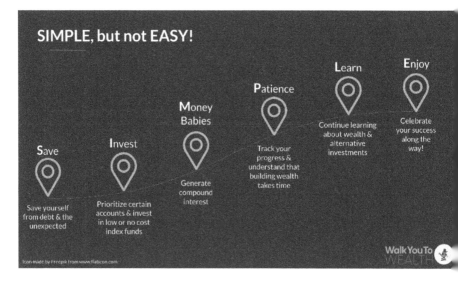

I will discuss each of these steps in detail through personal stories about my successes and failures as well as supporting data. Let me start by saying that these steps are indeed "simple;" however, they are not easy. What I mean is that I will break down each of these steps into simplistic actions that you can take, but completing the actions is the most important and also the hardest part. It requires some of your time, willingness to make trade-offs, personal sacrifice, patience, and potentially some behavioral changes, to ultimately develop a sound financial foundation. Following these steps has allowed me to grow my net worth significantly, and I am convinced that they can, and should, be implemented by anyone who wants to change their relationship with money from one where instead of working for it, it works for you.

You may already be thinking that this sounds complicated or only something for rich people, and if so, you are partially right. The world of personal finance is complicated due to the volume of choices, our own human behavior, and the fact that there are very few agreements between so-called experts. Again, the intent of this book isn't to be perfect, as much as I personally would love if there were a perfect solution, it's simply to be better! Now that we have introductions out of the way, it's time to take our first step together!

Chapter One: SIMPLE Step 1 - Save Yourself from Debt & the Unexpected

"Everyone has a plan until they get punched in the mouth."

Mike Tyson

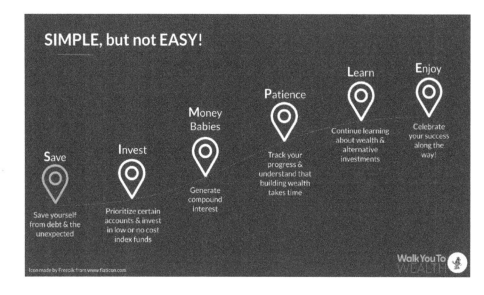

"Call 911" I remember my wife saying through a forced calm voice from across the room. Words no one ever wants to hear, especially a parent. My wife and I had just awoken to the sound of our 5-year-old struggling to breathe. We brought my son downstairs so as not to wake his younger brother and waited for help, all the while trying to remain calm, which was fairly impossible, so as not to panic our little guy even more. When the ambulance arrived, they quickly assessed that it was the croup which is an infection that obstructs breathing, causes a seal-like barking cough, but is not serious or life threatening. I am forever grateful that this scary incident turned out to be an innocuous event. To be safe, we went to the hospital. I rode in the back of the ambulance with my son, and we talked about anything other than the situation to keep him calm. We talked about all the equipment, the lights, and how his little brother would be jealous that he got to ride in an ambulance. At the hospital, he was given some steroids to help him breathe and a popsicle (he still talks about that popsicle!). The second I realized he was going to be okay, I remember thinking "how much is this going to cost me?" I'm not proud that this was my second thought, but it was. I was trying to calculate in my head the cost of the ambulance ride, which isn't priced as easily as one from Uber, the steroids, and even the damn popsicle. If at this time in my life, I had a dedicated emergency fund, I likely wouldn't have thought of the financial aspect of this situation until a month later when I received the bill.

This story brings us to the first step on our journey together, which is arguably the most boring, but also the most important. Think about building a house, this is pouring our cement foundation so that everything above it doesn't crumble to the ground. This is about creating a separate account that is only for emergencies, such as a job loss, or a medical issue like the one I just described with my son. You should pretend this account doesn't exist once it's funded, except for reviewing it on an annual basis to determine if the amount is still reasonable based on your current lifestyle. More on the amount in a minute, but first let's discuss the account. The money should be in an account that is insured by the Federal Deposit Insurance Corporation (FDIC) or the Securities Investor Protection Corporation (SIPC), which you can find at a number of free providers, such as Charles Schwab, Vanguard, Fidelity Investments, online banks, such as Ally or Marcus by Goldman Sachs, or your local bank. For a list of insured accounts, I would Google options at any of the providers mentioned above and after a few clicks you should have a free and insured account for your emergency savings. The interest rate on this account will largely be irrelevant, given that this is not meant to be an investment, but rather, savings. Savings are intended to be readily available for a stated purpose, such as an emergency in this case, while investments are not intended to be readily available in the short-term as they are designed to meet their purpose, such as retirement, in the long-term. The most important features of an emergency account are that it is insured by the FDIC or SIPC and that it's free.

In terms of the amount in your emergency fund, I would recommend $100-$500, if you have any credit card debt. I will discuss credit cards in a minute, but for now, just know this is your target amount. If it feels overwhelming given your personal situation, then try to break it down into a weekly or daily amount. For example, if you are trying to save $100 over the course of a month, it would be equivalent to saving $25 a week, or approximately $3 a day. This obviously doesn't change the goal of $100; however, from a psychological perspective, it's easier for us to gain momentum with small steps. You may also be wondering why I would recommend any amount of money to be saved in this account if you have credit card debt, but my logic is simple. There will always be something that happens unexpectedly, a trip to the emergency room, a flat tire, a broken appliance, etc. and having some money in this account will prevent you from adding to your credit card debt when it does.

Next, let's discuss credit cards. Let's start by getting rid of the myth that credit cards are evil. If used responsibly, and that's a big "IF," credit cards provide protection from fraudulent charges, as well as convenience and rewards. I use my credit card for most purchases and recurring bills, I pay my balance in full every month, and earn 2% cash back. In summary, I make all the purchases that I would normally make and essentially get paid 2% to do it, which is deposited directly into my emergency fund. For me, this equates to over $1,500 per year that's added to my emergency fund for free! Now that doesn't sound evil! That being said, it's the convenience of credit cards where the negative side effects appear. It is so easy to spend more than what you can afford, unlike using cash to pay for everything, like Mims did, which is exactly what the credit card company wants you to do. If you are in credit card debt, you are not alone.

Last year, my wife and I found out that my in-laws, who are in their late 70s, had $90,000 of credit card debt. Shocked would be a significant understatement! Given my background, I offered to help dig through their financial information to chart a path out of debt. It's hard not to be judgmental in that situation as I'm seeing the stress on my wife's face while combing through monthly statements filled with Starbucks coffees and Target runs. Fortunately, my in-laws were able to climb out of debt; however, it wasn't without significant sacrifice, including moving to a cheaper apartment complex, selling assets, and seemingly losing the gold part of their "golden" years. I also witnessed firsthand the toll it takes on your family when you're not financially sound. My wife is still dealing with the ramifications, including the emotional toll of the situation, and a feeling of apprehension every time the phone rings or a text message pings from her parents. As a result, we've had many long discussions about how we would never put our children through something like that, and it served as a hard reminder that your personal financial troubles aren't always just yours and can significantly impact those around you. My in-laws' debt, while shocking to us, is all too common, with the average credit card debt in the United States being approximately $6,000, but before we get into amounts, interest, and payment strategies, let's try to look at this situation from a slightly different perspective. Let's change the narrative from a problem to an opportunity.

What if I told you that paying off your credit card debt will generate the highest guaranteed return that I've ever found in my time investing? In other words, change your vantage point from a debtor to an investor, and not only an investor, but an investor who is about to potentially make their greatest investment. Before you dismiss my thinking, allow me to explain further. The average credit card interest rate is approximately 22% and so by paying off your credit card debt you are earning a guaranteed 22% return. To put that in context; that is more than double the historical average return of the U.S. stock market, which is not guaranteed, and anywhere from 10X-20X the return on other guaranteed investments. In other words, paying off this type of debt is a great "investment."

There are two primary methods of paying off credit card debt: the snowball approach, and the avalanche approach. The latter involves targeting the debt with the highest interest rate. For example, let's say you have the following five credit cards, balances, and interest rates:

Card	Balance	Interest Rate
Visa	$3,000	15%
American Express	$1,500	16%
Best Buy (store card)	$750	18%
Amazon (store card)	$250	14%
Target (store card)	$125	15%

If you followed the avalanche approach, you would work towards paying off the Best Buy (store card) from the example because it is charging you the highest rate of interest at 18%, therefore, representing the best investment return. Once that card is paid off, you would move to the next highest interest rate, or the American Express card in our example. This is mathematically the "right" approach, but as I said earlier, this walk to wealth isn't about perfection, which is why I would recommend the snowball approach.

Using the snowball approach, you would pay off the credit cards in the order of balance, from lowest to highest. In our example above, you would pay them off in the reverse order they are listed, starting first with the Target (store card) which has the smallest balance of $125 and then moving up the list to the Amazon (store card). This will not provide the initial 18% return of the avalanche method above, but from a psychological perspective you are more likely to keep climbing the mountain because you are making progress faster. Let's say you can afford to pay an extra $15 per month towards your debt, the Target (store card) can be eliminated in less than 9 months, where it would take 50 months or over 4 years to pay off the Best Buy (store card) from the avalanche approach. Again, this is about giving you a better approach that actually works as opposed to one that's perfect on paper, but nearly impossible to implement. This will take time and it won't be easy, but think about the "investment" you are making and the interest you are "earning." If you are concerned about not being able to afford this investment, whether it's $15 like in our example or more, I have some ideas where you can find the money which I will cover in the next chapter.

If you are not in credit card debt, I recommend that your emergency fund have three to six months of essential expenses such as mortgage, food, clothing, and/or rent. I would recommend three months of essential expenses if you have multiple income sources in your house, such as a working spouse, or if you work in a safe profession. There are very few safe professions these days, but a tenured teacher or federal judge are two examples. Feeling safe in your job is not the same as a safe job. On the other hand, I would recommend six months of essential expenses be saved if you have a single income source or work in a less secure field, like most of us. Bottom line is that you need to start with an emergency fund, which may vary in size, but generally consists of three to six months of essential expenses which will help prevent a financial catastrophe when the unexpected occurs, and it always does.

SIMPLE STEP 1 – SUMMARY OF ACTIONS (SAFE)

At this point in our walk, you may be feeling discouraged by the idea of saving three to six months of essential expenses for an emergency fund or "investing" in your credit card debt. I understand, but the most important thing to do now is take a deep breath, implement the relevant actions below so that your financial foundation is SAFE, and then let's figure out how we can find some money to fund this first SIMPLE step.

- **S**tart - Simply taking your first step gets us moving on our walk to wealth.

- Account Opening - Open an FDIC or SIPC insured account at a no cost provider such as Fidelity Investments, Charles Schwab, Ally, Vanguard, Marcus, or your local bank (some may require an initial deposit or direct deposit).

- Fund your greatest investment - If you have credit card debt, work on saving $100-$500 in your emergency account, breaking it down into daily amounts to make progress. Then, tackle your first and potentially most lucrative guaranteed investment by using the snowball method to pay off your debt.

- Emergency savings - If you don't have any credit card debt, start to accumulate three to six months of essential expenses in your emergency account.

CHAPTER ONE AND A HALF: I CAN'T AFFORD STEP 1

"I love money. I love everything about it. I bought some pretty good stuff. Got me a $300 pair of socks. Got a fur sink. An electric dog polisher. A gasoline powered turtleneck sweater. And, of course, I bought some dumb stuff, too."

Steve Martin

Hopefully you are feeling good about our first SIMPLE step, but if you are like most people I meet, you are likely feeling overwhelmed. You might be thinking "Sounds great Kevin, but is the money going to magically appear to pay off my debt and create my emergency fund?" or "So, is this the inevitable chapter about budgeting where I close the book and allow it to collect dust on the floor for a few months?" The short answers are: yes, the money will appear, but a magic hat isn't necessary, and no, I am not going to discuss budgeting. I have two reasons for not talking about budgets: 1) I don't use one, and so it would be wildly hypocritical of me to talk you into using one (I have been called many things in my life, but never a hypocrite!), and 2) they don't work for most of us. Now, if you are one of the rare breeds who budget successfully, then I certainly encourage you to keep up the good work. If, on the other hand, you are like me, a budget is useless. This is the same reason that diets and working out rarely work over a long period of time. I'm sure there is a fancy psychological term

27

for this, but let's call it old-fashioned laziness. There is nothing wrong with that, very few of us want to diet, workout, or budget. In this case, we can get to where we are going without it, by having an investment plan which we will discuss later, but first, let's talk about how we magically make this money appear. There are only two sides of this equation, we can figure out a way to lower expenses and/or increase earnings. Lowering expenses is finite, in that, if you are spending $1,000 per month, you can only possibly save $1,000 per month by eliminating all your spending, but the other side of the equation, earning more, is limitless.

Let's start on the expense side of the equation and talk about spending intentionally. Spending intentionally is being aware of where your money is going, regardless of how it may seem to others. For example, I have a ridiculously expensive pair of American Giant sweatpants which retail for $100. This seems even more outrageous in written form! Are they expensive? Yes. Did I spend that money intentionally? Yes. This second question is the key. I wear my American Giant sweatpants almost every day after work. They are warm, comfortable, and have lasted for years. Short story, I value being comfortable and am willing to spend on it.

If you want a more extreme example of spending intentionally, how about one that cost more than $500,000? This was the decision that my wife and I made when we had our first child and she quit her job as an elementary school teacher to stay home and raise our son, and eventually our second child too. Our decision to forgo her income for over

10 years was an easy one, despite the huge cost, financial sacrifice, and risk that came with it. It was an easy and quick decision because it was important to both of us, and we felt strongly about it. Looking back, neither of us would do it differently for our family and this is what spending intentionally is all about. A pair of expensive sweatpants or having one spouse stay home may not be how you want to spend your money, but I hope that my examples provide some context for what it means to spend intentionally, both on a small and large scale.

Now that isn't to say that you can claim everything you are spending money on is intentional. When my kids were in the second grade, they learned about needs vs. wants, which is a lesson that should be taught to adults. How many times have you heard a colleague, friend, or family member say they "need" a vacation or "deserve" a night out? I find that people who typically make statements like this are those who know deep down that they can't afford to spend money on that vacation or night out, so they tell themselves they "need" or "deserve" it. The items we need are fairly basic and include food, clothing, water, air, and shelter. If you think about this short list, it doesn't cost very much, including one of the five being completely free. When my wife was teaching, there was a family in the school who was struggling financially, and the principal kindly organized a fundraiser. By all accounts, this family couldn't provide some of the basic necessities, including clothing for their elementary aged son. The school raised a significant amount of money and other donations for the family, which was great. After the fundraiser, my wife got to know the child a little better, and he would regularly discuss his weekends which primarily consisted of playing their new video game system on their 65-inch TV. I only tell this story because it's all too common. Before you spend a dollar intentionally on anything, whether it be a vacation, a night out, a huge TV, or a pair of great sweatpants, you need to have your basic necessities covered.

In practice, what this all means for me is that I try to recognize what my "needs" really are and limit my wants to items or experiences that I am intentionally spending on. For every pair of American Giant sweatpants, there are countless items that I choose not to purchase, or spend significantly less on, because they don't matter as much to me. For example, I choose to spend as little as possible on cars, more on that later, shoes, and dress clothes. My sneakers literally have holes in them, I only buy dress clothes when required, typically a wedding or funeral, and I drive an 11-year-old Chevy Equinox. It's not about being able to "afford" new shoes, a better car, or dress clothes, but rather, that I don't value them highly in comparison to other items, like my sweatpants! For those of you who value everything, I take back what I said about a budget, you do need one!

With that said, it is not always easy to spot the "unintentional" expenses that we have. These are the ones that we don't really think about. Some people might say that these expenses are not a big deal, and they don't really matter. However, when you look at it from a different perspective, you can see how these small expenses can add up and become something much bigger. Here are a few that we can potentially eliminate or reduce and then reallocate that money towards our first SIMPLE step; Save.

Online Promotions - We can't spend a minute online without being bombarded with ads. To make matters worse, these ads are targeted to us individually using algorithms. For example, when I recently started searching for new luggage to replace our newlywed set that's about 20 years old, I started seeing luggage ads on every site and even in my Gmail inbox. This makes impulse purchasing harder to deal with. The second you Google anything, every company on the internet wants to sell it to you. We also receive countless email and text promotions, and this was one of my biggest weaknesses several years ago. For me, it was the Amazon Deals of the Day email. I spent so much money on useless items, like a blender and waffle iron, because they were on "sale" and could be purchased with two-clicks from my inbox. This is the new and more expensive version of the old adage about not food shopping when you're hungry. Unfortunately, there appears little we can do to stop receiving targeted ads as long as we want to keep using the internet, and I'm not an extremist. That being said, one action that may help is to unsubscribe to as many of these email notifications as possible. How many of these do you receive from companies where you made a one-time purchase and signed up to receive texts or email notifications for some 10-15% discount? Now, your one-time purchase may be costing you a lot more as you've become a repeat customer whenever you open these targeted emails or texts.

Manage Subscriptions | Update Profile | Unsubscribe

Here is what we need to do, find and click on the very small font at the bottom of your next email that says "Unsubscribe," pictured below:

This is similar for texts which typically ask you to text back "unsubscribe" or "stop" to remove yourself from the list. Even if you pay full price for that new waffle iron when you need it, you likely will have saved money on the dozens of other items you bought in the meantime.

Cell Phones and Plans - Cell phones are a cheaper version of a car from the standpoint that most of us need one, but we replace them too soon and also pay for more service than we need. The only way I've found to save money on the phone itself is to use it as long as it will last beyond your payment plan and avoid falling into the trap of "needing" a new phone every two years when the next iPhone or Pixel is released. We all likely have a friend who claims they can't afford some actual necessity, like insurance or medicine, and tells you this via a text from their latest iPhone. I'm an Android user, and only recently upgraded my phone when it literally stopped working and was also no longer receiving security updates. The phone was certainly slow, and the battery was terrible towards the end, but for approximately $1,000 per phone, I will wait until I need one before replacing it. I will also upgrade to a better model, but not the newest. In other words, when everyone is buying the Pixel 12, I will be upgrading to the 10 or 11.

Now onto my biggest pet peeve around cell phones, cell phone plans. A few years ago, my wife and I were paying approximately $120 per month for our cellular service with Verizon and are now paying approximately $45 per month with GoogleFi. That's a savings of almost $80 per month! This is not an advertisement or endorsement for GoogleFi, although I am a happy customer. The point is to shop around and find a provider where you pay for what you need. The reason that GoogleFi is so much cheaper for us is that we only pay for the data that we actually use, and we are hyper aware of using Wi-Fi where available, which is almost everywhere these days. I also used to listen to podcasts and audiobooks during my two-hour commute but would download them before I left the house to avoid paying for unnecessary data. You may be thinking "Well, I have an unlimited plan, so who cares about the data usage?" Do you really need that unlimited plan though? Look at your data usage, try to use less, and shop around for a low-cost provider who can offer you great service at a reasonable price.

Subscription Services - I am guilty of this one myself, and as I said earlier, I am not a hypocrite! Everything in our world today seems to be billed as a subscription which is just a marketing ploy to make it seem affordable and to play into our general laziness. Below are some of the most common subscriptions and their approximate costs as of the publication of this book:

Entertainment:

- Amazon Prime: ~$13/month

- Netflix: ~$15/month

- Disney Plus: ~$8/month

- Amazon Music, Apple Music, Spotify Premium: ~$10/month

- YouTube TV: ~$65/month

Food:

- Meal Prep (e.g., Home Chef, Sun basket): ~$300-$500/month (assuming two people and four meals per week)

Fitness:

- Gym: ~$40/month

- Peloton: ~$13/month

The list could go on and on, and as I mentioned above, I am more than guilty of participating in a few of these. You should start by gathering your last few months of bank and credit card statements to see your recurring charges. You may pay for some of the above or potentially different subscriptions, and my point is not to eliminate all of these services and live like a hermit, but rather, to review your subscription spending and figure out if this is how you intentionally want to spend your money.

For example, let's assume you are making $15 per hour at your job, and you are paying for Netflix. That essentially means that you are working for almost two hours a month (once you factor in taxes) to pay for Netflix. Another way to look at this cost is over the course of a year, which equates to approximately three full days of work at $15 per hour and a total cost of $180. Is that worth it to you? If so, great and move on to the next one. If not, cancel it and continue down your list of subscriptions. Personally, I continually fall into this trap, which is why I periodically review these costs. During my last review, my wife and I found that we were no longer watching Netflix and so we canceled it. It would have been easy to say, "It's only $15," or "We can afford it," but that's $180 a year that I could use differently. Damn you, laziness! My last word on subscriptions, is that the above are examples, so please don't read the list and say, "This doesn't apply to me because I don't pay for any of these," or "Why does Kevin hate Netflix so much?" These are only examples, and we are increasingly living in a world of subscriptions because companies want to take advantage of our laziness and have the benefit of more predictable revenue streams. I have no problem with companies doing this either, as it also makes it easier to cancel these services, but we need to be aware of them and review these subscriptions periodically to make sure we are spending intentionally. With that, I will hop off my soapbox and move to our next big category: Cars.

Cars – Would you spend $30,000 on something that was virtually guaranteed to lose approximately $6,000 of value during the first 12 months? I'm hoping that I led the witness on this one and your answer was "absolutely not." That being said, every day I walk and drive past hundreds of luxury cars which cost a lot more than $30,000 and at least some of which are being driven by people who can't afford them. For those who can afford them, I would still ask "Why?" as cars are the only asset I know of that immediately lose value the second they are purchased, but as I mentioned earlier, the idea here is to spend intentionally, and if this is something you value then let's cut elsewhere.

At this point, you are likely frustrated and thinking, "So, this bozo is telling me to walk to work, school, the grocery store, etc." I am not telling you that. I am simply pointing out that cars are expensive and should be viewed as an asset, in most cases a necessary asset, but an asset, nevertheless. Most of us wouldn't buy a house if it were guaranteed to lose 50% of its value in 5 years! So, what should you do? Personally, I still buy new cars, but I purchase the base model of a car that is significantly under what I can afford, and I drive it for as long as it will last. By comparison, the average length of a car loan is slightly longer than the average time of ownership. Think about that for a minute. On average, we are paying for cars longer than we actually own them, or, said differently, we never actually own them at all, but rather, move on to the next car and are forever paying for a new and rapidly depreciating asset.

As I am writing this book, I am driving a 2011 Chevy Equinox with 90k miles on it. The car is fully paid for, and I will hopefully drive it for many more years. Below are a few practical options:

- Buy used;

- If you live in a city, leverage public transportation, a bike, or when necessary, rideshare apps, like Lyft and Uber;

- Carpool to extend the life of your car (Waze, among other apps has a feature for this);

- Work remotely, if possible; and

- In a multi-car family, like mine, figure out if having one car is feasible.

Prior to having kids, my wife and I lived in Boston, and we were a one car family, and I walked to work. The health and financial benefits were enormous. When we had kids and moved to the burbs, I commuted an hour each way to work, but now, after years of commuting, I am fully remote, and although we have two cars, I will likely be able to extend the use of my car by eight-to-ten years given the low mileage that I now drive. If you take one thing from this section, it should be that cars are often necessary in our society, but they are also expensive and depreciate rapidly, so buy cheaply, cautiously, and extend the life as long as possible.

Housing - *Drip, drop, drip, drop,* I remember waking up to the pitter patter of rain, *drip, drop, drip, drop,* in my CLOSET! This was about three months after my wife and I purchased our home. After multiple buckets, several estimates, and $10,000, we were the lucky owners of a new roof. I could fill an entire book with stories like this about my house. For those of you who are old enough to have seen the classic movie Money Pit with Tom Hanks, that's a mild version of what we've been through! This is all to say that homes are expensive, and you need to be prepared if you decide to purchase one. So, let's get prepared by talking about size, staying power, and how much you can afford!

Now, I will fall on my sword again. My house is too big for my family. It was one of the smallest houses for sale in the area we wanted to move to at the time, but I still wish it had one less bedroom and a smaller yard. Real estate can be a great investment, which I will cover later in this book, but when you are buying a primary residence don't fall into the "bigger is always better" trap. For example, I pay $5,000 a year for landscaping (don't judge me, this is part of my intentional spending!) and whether it's your time, mowing your own grass for example, your money, or both, bigger is not always better, but it is always more expensive! From a statistical perspective, we only use a fraction of our home's square footage as illustrated below, by this study from UCLA:

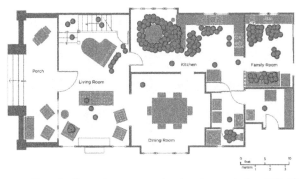

In terms of why we use so little of our houses, that's simple. According to research, the average size of new homes in the United States has doubled since 1960, while the average number of people per household has decreased. Specifically, the average square footage has increased 105% (1960: 1,200 square feet, 2020: 2,464 square feet), while the average number of people per household has decreased 24% (1960: 3.33 people, 2020: 2.53 people). Let's quickly put these stats together. The average amount of square footage per person was 360 in 1960 and increased 170%, to 973, by 2020! This is more square footage per person than the total of my first two-bedroom condo in Boston! I'm tired of math now, but hopefully the point is clear that a home is one of the most expensive purchases you will ever make, and you should think carefully about how much house you "need."

Now that we know bigger isn't always better, but is always more expensive, let's talk about time of ownership. A home purchase is expensive and can be a good store of wealth for most people, if you decide to remain in your home for a long time. I personally recommend following my ten-year rule as a general guideline:

1. Question: Do you plan on staying in this home for ten years or more?

   a. Context: I would seriously consider renting if you don't think you can commit to at least ten years given the size of the purchase and housing market fluctuations.

2. Question: Could you reasonably pay off this home in ten years?

   a. Context: This does not mean that you *should* pay off your home in ten years (more on this, later), it simply means that the amount you can afford to borrow over a 30-year mortgage may well exceed what you could pay off in 10 years. In other words, if the purchase price of your house is $300,000, could you afford to pay it off in ten years? More quick math; if you put 20% down and borrowed $240,000 at 3%, that would bring your monthly payment to approximately $1,000 per month, and if you wanted to it pay it off in 10 years you would have to add another $1,300 per month for a total payment of $2,300 per month. Again, I am not suggesting that you pay off your house in ten years, merely using this method to figure out what is affordable without stretching yourself too far. In order to do this math yourself, you can simply Google extra mortgage payment calculators. This will help ensure that you don't overextend yourself and that you have money for general maintenance and improvements which is minimally 1% per year of your home's value, or in our example $3,000 per year, or in my case $10,000 in three months for a new roof!

In summary, the items above were not meant to be an exhaustive list of ways to cut unintentional expenses, but hopefully, at this point on our walk, you have realized that you can afford to build an emergency fund or pay off credit card debt by spending more intentionally which may mean canceling some subscription services, switching cell phone plans, not falling prey to targeted promotions, extending the life of your car, renting instead of buying a home, and/or buying a smaller home.

Now, we know how to spend intentionally, so let's focus on the other side of the equation, earning more income. There are two primary options here, and they are not mutually exclusive, again, this is the limitless side of the equation. The first option is to focus on earning more from your job, and the second is one of the most overused terms in all of personal finance: "side hustle." This section will be quick and painless, much like how my two boys will literally wait for me to remove their band aids instead of asking my wife. There are tons of low qualification "side hustles" or part–time jobs in our current economy that you can take advantage of to earn money for your emergency fund and/or to pay off credit card debt, and below are a few of those options:

- Rideshare: If you have a car, license, and can pass a background check, you may be able to drive for Uber or Lyft in your spare time.

- Food Delivery: Similar to the above, you could deliver food through one of the many companies that specialize in this, including UberEats or DoorDash.

- Cleaning Services: There are many apps, such as Thumbtack, which help homeowners find cleaners which require minimal qualifications.

- Dog Walking: You could use an app like Wag or Rover to find people in your neighborhood who will pay you to walk their dogs.

- Gig Economy: If you have some technical ability (e.g., editing, logo design) you can outsource those skills to millions of people through sites and apps like Fiverr.

- Create a Product: If you have the ability or skill to make a product that others want to buy you can sell it through a site like Etsy.

- Virtual Tutor: If you have an area of expertise, a laptop, and an internet connection you could potentially tutor through a site like Varsity Tutors.

Similarly, to our conversation on spending intentionally, the above is not meant to be an all-inclusive list, and if you want more ideas, you can Google the most overused term in personal finance, "side hustle," for thousands of blog posts and articles on the topic. Now, let's discuss what, in my opinion, is the most lucrative way to earn more, which is by focusing on your job and skills. For me, the following has had infinitely more financial impact than any of the above "side hustles" could have. During my career, I've earned an average compensation increase of approximately 20% per year and I've been able to do it by keeping the BALL in my court:

- **Be** Great - We all have inherent and natural abilities that we need to tap into in order to be great at our job. Unfortunately, we spend too much time focusing on trying to improve our weaknesses instead of concentrating on these natural strengths. Personally, I am a great people manager. During my career in financial services, I regularly scored in the top 10% of all managers at the company I worked for, which at its peak had over 60k employees. This is something that I naturally did well, because I am willing to give honest feedback, but also care deeply about the development of my team. Any member of my team would tell you that there was a family type atmosphere that I was able to create organically. I am naturally charismatic, personable, honest, and most importantly authentic, all of which helped me to be a great manager. During my first review after being given the opportunity to manage people, my manager noticed my ability and said, "Your team will run through walls for you." This isn't something I set out to cultivate, but rather a marketable skill that I excelled at without much effort. Since that time, I've put in more work to become an even better people manager and to further strengthen my natural ability. My point is not to be a great people manager, but rather find out what you naturally do better than most other people and focus on being great at that!

- Ask - Despite the last section on my "greatness," I don't like asking for promotions or raises, but it's a critical step. The number of employees who I've witnessed receive a promotion or raise because they asked is huge. Now, this doesn't mean you should just walk into your manager's office and ask. You need to develop a plan. The most successful "asks" that I've received have involved three things: good timing, potential leverage, and quantifiable information. In terms of timing, you want to start having the conversation with your manager about six months before your annual performance cycle. This will give both of you adequate time to discuss it, but not too much time that you lose momentum. In an ideal world, you also have some leverage. This doesn't mean that you threaten to leave, as loyalty is highly valued in my opinion, but rather you have leverage because of your greatness that we just discussed. You have a unique quality or skill that makes you valuable. Lastly, you should have some quantifiable information. In my example, being in the top 10% of all managers was easily quantifiable. In your case, it may mean that you increased production of widgets by 20%. I've been on both sides of this situation, as an employee and a manager, and a well-articulated, well-timed ask will often lead to a raise or promotion.

- Leave - I spent 15 years at one company and there were lots of benefits to that level of consistency; however, I was always willing to leave for the right opportunity. During my time there, I always accepted phone calls from recruiters and even applied and interviewed for several jobs. Eventually, a recruiter from a cryptocurrency exchange reached out to me on LinkedIn and I found a job that I was finally willing to leave for. The national average raise for a new job is approximately 15%. That's a huge increase, but you have to be willing to leave.

- Learn - You should always be adding to your skill set. Part of my ability to earn more money is directly tied to my "paper" qualifications. These include an MBA and multiple professional certifications. These cost money to obtain, but some employers will reimburse you for some, or all, of the expense. Additionally, there are so many free options to learn new skills through colleges and universities, including the Ivy Leagues, who openly share some of their course materials for free along with sites like YouTube, Coursera, and others. Lastly, I'm an avid reader or, as my kids would say, "listener" because I enjoy audiobooks. I use my local library to get access to free audiobooks which I used to listen to during my commute and now listen to during my morning walk around the neighborhood before signing in for remote work. The paper qualifications may help to substantiate your learning or validate your accomplishment, but there are lots of ways to learn new and marketable skills.

SIMPLE Step 1 - Summary of Actions (SET)

In summary, the following actions will SET you up to complete the first SIMPLE step, Save, on our walk to wealth:

- Spend Intentionally - Spending intentionally will lead to less waste and increased happiness.

- Earn More - Earning more is limitless and can be used to fund emergencies, debt payments, and when we get to it, investments.

- Time Matters - If you are making a significant purchase, such as a home or car, or even a smaller one, such as a cell phone, plan to own it for long time, in the case of a home and car, at least 10 years, and in the case of a cell phone, at least three years.

Chapter Two: SIMPLE Step 2 – Invest

"The biggest risk of all is not taking one."

Mellody Hobson

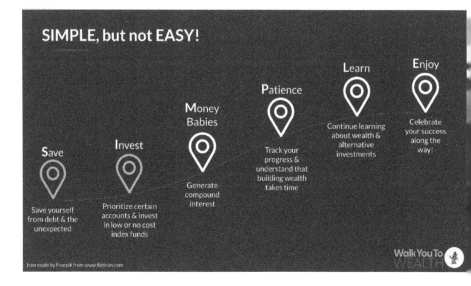

If you think that investing seems too complicated, then great minds think alike. Investing is way too complicated, overwhelming, and intimidating. A few years ago, my oldest brother texted me to ask what my sister-in-law should do with a 401k from a previous employer. When I replied that she should roll it into her new 401k plan or into a Traditional IRA (if you have no idea what a Traditional IRA is, you are not alone, and I will cover that later, but for now, just know that it's a type of investment account) at a company like Fidelity Investments or Vanguard his question was "Will Fidelity open a small account?" My response was "YES!" My brother had the same misconception that most people do, that investing and opening accounts at traditional financial services firms like Fidelity Investments, Vanguard, or Charles Schwab is only for rich people; however, the reality is that you can open an account with as little as you can afford. The point, and my hope, is that by the end of this book you won't be intimidated.

At most financial services firms, the process of opening an account is similar to opening any other type of account online. You can easily do it from the comfort of your couch, which should minimize the fear factor. Thanks to my sister-in-law, we know that anyone can open an account, but what type of account? Here is where the financial services industry makes my head spin. The first thing to know is that there is no such thing as a perfect account, as each one has unique benefits. Additionally, the accounts are labeled with non-intuitive acronyms like IRA, or a series of letters and numbers that are meaningless to you and me, like 401k, 403b, or 457. We also have "taxable brokerage accounts," which may lead you to believe that the other accounts are tax-free, but they generally aren't. Let's leave behind some of this noise by putting accounts into the following four easy categories based on their tax treatment:

1. Never - Pay Taxes Never

2. Now - Pay Taxes Now

3. Later - Pay Taxes Later

4. Always - Pay Taxes Always

In general, the more tax benefits or advantages for a given account, the more rules, restrictions, or limited eligibility that exists. Let's walk through each of these account types in more detail below and then I will cover how to prioritize them:

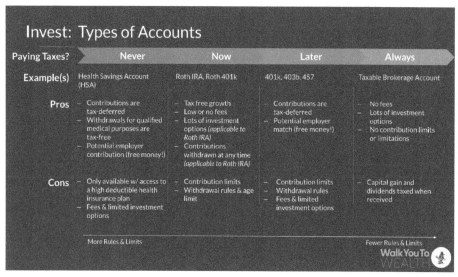

Never Account - The only investment account that I know of, which can potentially allow you to never pay taxes is a Health Savings Account or HSA. HSAs can be a terrific retirement investment vehicle. For one, your contributions are tax deductible and withdrawals for qualified medical purposes are tax-free. Let's stop here and think about this overly complicated sentence. All it means is that you can potentially never pay taxes, hence the more intuitive category of "Never." You may be thinking one of two things: "Sounds great, where do I sign up?" or "I won't need money for medical expenses so who cares?" If you are thinking the former, you are only eligible for an HSA if you also have access to a high deductible health plan for your medical insurance. This type of insurance comes with one potential downside of needing to pay for most non-preventative medical treatments out of your own pocket; however, the significant upside is being able to invest and never pay taxes on your contributions or the investment earnings. This is especially key if you are young, healthy, and can financially afford to pay for a rare non-preventative medical appointment or treatment. These types of accounts often come with an employer contribution too, which makes them even better! A quick pro tip for those interested, save your receipts. You can withdraw from an HSA for prior out of pocket qualified medical expenses (refer to the IRS.gov site for what falls into this definition) regardless of the time-period. In other words, I can withdraw money tax-free in five years for my prescription glasses that I purchased today. This allows your HSA to potentially be used prior to a normal retirement age if you save your receipts. For the latter point about potentially not needing money for medical costs, this is one of the largest expenses in retirement. Per Fidelity Investments,[iii] in 2021 an average retired couple age 65 may need approximately $300,000 saved (after-tax) to cover health care expenses. Now, best case scenario, you are the healthiest person in the world in retirement and never need glasses, contacts, surgery, private health insurance, etc., what happens to your money? Simple, it's still your money and after age 65 you can withdraw it for any purpose; however, you will lose the "Never" aspect and will have to pay income taxes, similar to a "Later" account. Due to the fact that these accounts are generally tied to an employer, there may be account fees (typically minimal) associated with account maintenance and your investment options may be limited. We will cover fees and investment options later, but for now, I'm simply trying to lay out the pros and cons of the "Never" account. In summary, the downsides of the "Never" account is that access to one is dependent on your health insurance, investment options may be limited, you need to be able to afford current medical related expenses that aren't covered, and account fees may be applicable; however, the upside is potentially "Never" paying taxes and also receiving an employer contribution.

Now Account - The "Now" account is a Roth IRA account, by its given name. In this case, you are contributing after-tax dollars (not that great), but your investment will grow tax-free and can be withdrawn after age 59.5 for any reason you want. These "Now" accounts are great if you are young and have time to allow your money to grow for retirement (if you have no idea how your money "grows" don't worry, we will cover that later too!). These accounts also allow you to use the money for other qualified purposes prior to age 59.5 without paying a penalty, such as education or up to $10,000 for a first-time home purchase. You can also withdraw your contributions, not your earnings, penalty free at any time. These accounts are typically fee free, allow access to a wide variety of investment options, and do not have "Minimum Required Distributions" which is just a way for the government to force you to withdraw money at a certain age. In summary, tax-free growth, no account fees, ability to withdraw contributions at any time, lots of investment options, and freedom to decide when or if to withdraw after age 59.5. The downsides are that you are only eligible if you earn less than a certain amount which is periodically adjusted by the IRS. At the time of this book, you need to earn less than $198,000 if you file your taxes as married or $125,000 if filing single, but you should Google "IRS Roth IRA income limits" for current information. The other downside is that you are limited in terms of how much you can contribute to this account. This also changes periodically, but has been approximately $6,000 per year for the last several years. A quick side note on a cousin of the Roth IRA, which is the Roth 401k. The Roth 401k is similar in that it allows tax-free growth; however, it differs in that the income limit isn't applicable and the contribution limit is higher. It is also only offered through an employer sponsored plan, unlike the Roth IRA which can be opened by any individual, regardless of employment. The higher contribution limit of the Roth 401k will come at the expense of contributing to a "Later" account which we will discuss next.

Later Accounts - The "Later" accounts, such as a 401k, 403b, or 457, allow you to defer taxes until retirement when you could be in a lower tax bracket. I say, "Could be," because no one can predict tax rates and even if you could jump into your DeLorean and get a hold of the 2050 tax brackets like Biff with the Sports Almanac in *Back to The*

Future II, you would also need to know your income in 2050. That being said, as Wimpy repeated so often in *Popeye* "I'll gladly pay you Tuesday for a hamburger today." You are getting a guaranteed deferral of taxes today, with the promise to pay them later. These accounts may also include a company or employer contribution or match, which I will discuss more during the prioritization section, but for now the important key benefit is a guaranteed deferral of taxes today. The primary downsides of "Later" accounts are generally limited investment options, account fees which may be high, and you are capped by the IRS in terms of how much you can contribute, which has been approximately $20,000 in recent years (Google "401k contribution limit" for the current amount).

Always Account – The "Always" account is a taxable brokerage account, and it's one in which you can throw the rule book aside. Anything you want! There are no rules! You can contribute as much as you want, and your investment choices are seemingly limitless. The primary drawback of this account is my favorite five letter word, taxes. There are no tax benefits and the interest, dividends, and capital gains that you earn on this account will "always" be taxed when received. In other words, you contribute what you want, when you want, invest in almost anything, pay no fees, and also can withdraw what and when you want. The price of this flexibility is giving up any tax benefits. For this reason, we will want to be mindful of our investment choices for this account, which we will discuss later. Again, the purpose here is to simply understand the different types of accounts and their general features, benefits, and drawbacks.

Let's take a quick pause here to reflect on this section. We now know there are four basic types of accounts "Never, Now, Later, Always" based on the tax treatment of each. If you are feeling overwhelmed, take a deep breath, as we are going to go step-by-step through which accounts should be prioritized, but first, I wanted to make sure to cover the basic features of each type.

Once again, we are going to take this in small steps to make the walk to wealth easier. Now that you understand the basic types of accounts, you need to understand how to prioritize your money. Whether you have $25, $25,000, or $250,000, I want to help you make the most of your money. So, let's talk about the basics of prioritization (pictured below):

Invest: General Prioritization

Free Money	Never	Now	Later	Always
First priority is to get free money from your employer through a company contribution or matching program	Second priority is to "Never" pay taxes by investing in a Health Savings Account, which allows for tax deductible contributions and tax-free spending for qualified medical purposes	Third priority is to pay taxes "Now," invest the money, and let it grow tax-free through a Roth IRA	Fourth priority is to use a "Later" account to defer paying taxes until withdrawals in retirement at which time you could be in a lower tax bracket	Last priority is an "Always" account which is a taxable brokerage account which provides no limits on contributions or investment options; however, distributions will be taxed when received (more on this later)

Walk You To WEALTH

The first step is free money! I recently took my two children to buy a comic book at Newbury Comics, a local comic bookstore in my area. As the cashier was ringing up my Teen Titans comic, she mentioned that I was eligible to pick out another comic for free, based on their Buy-One-Get-One or BOGO sale. Now, I had a decision to make, walk back upstairs to the kid-friendly comic book section and get a completely FREE comic or leave (nothing like trying, but failing, to build suspense for an easy decision!). I immediately walked back upstairs with my two boys who were super excited to pick out a second comic book. The reason I tell you this story is that it's shocking how many people who have access to an employer contribution for their "Never" account (HSA) and/or their "Later" account (e.g., 401k, 403b) do not elect to open the account or don't contribute enough to receive the full company contribution or match. In other words, people leave the store instead of grabbing the free comic book! This is one of the rare times in life where there is such a thing as a free lunch. Does this really matter? Yes, it actually makes a huge difference over the long-term. Back to math! Let's take a basic example of a "Later" account match. For illustrative purposes, let's assume you earn $50,000 per year for 30 years, you never receive a raise, contribute 3% or $1,500 per year to your "Later" account, and your employer matches 3% or $1,500 per year, which is estimated to be the national average.

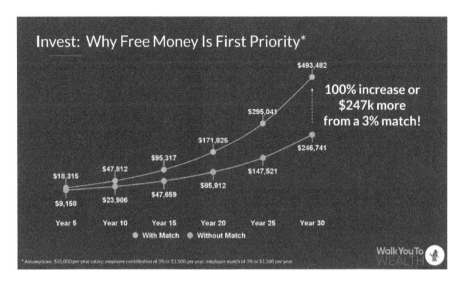

Invest: Why Free Money Is First Priority*

100% increase or $247k more from a 3% match!

$493,482
$295,041
$246,741
$171,825
$147,521
$95,317
$85,912
$47,812
$47,659
$18,315
$23,906
$9,158

Year 5   Year 10   Year 15   Year 20   Year 25   Year 30

● With Match   ● Without Match

* Assumptions: $50,000 per year salary; employee contribution of 3% or $1,500 per year; employer match of 3% or $1,500 per year

Walk You To WEALTH

After 30 years, you have almost $250,000 more from your employer match or a 100% increase! Not bad for a measly 3% or $1,500 per year. There are estimates that as many as 20% of people don't take advantage of this BOGO! If you are part of that 20%, stop reading, log in to your account, and adjust your contribution percentage now! Please also keep in mind that this illustration is based on a national average match of 3%, but during your next job search, you should use sites like Glassdoor.com, as well as company sites to target those that are more generous. Your retired self will thank you later. As an extreme example of generosity in this area, my former employer matched 7% and also contributed an additional 10% per year as part of a profit-sharing contribution. This is a life changing benefit

57

that many of us, including myself, when I first started working there at age 26, don't realize the full impact of.

The next prioritizations are in the same order as the accounts we previously discussed, Never, Now, Later, and Always. The primary reason for targeting them in this order are the tax advantages which we already discussed during the overview of each account type. In order to help crystallize the account prioritization process, below is a board game of questions that we will walk through:

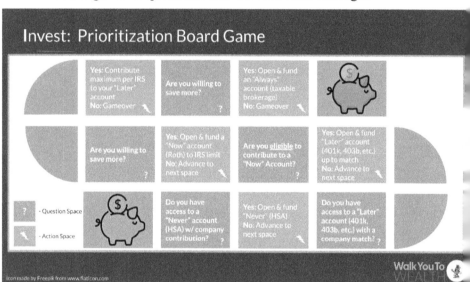

Let's play a game! My two boys, 10 and 8, aren't big fans of board games; however, they do enjoy playing the classic Candy Land. Playing Candy Land with them was the inspiration behind this next exercise that hopefully will cement our conversation about how to prioritize your accounts. The board game is made up of simple question and action spaces which you should move through in order. Below are details on the question and action spaces from the board game:

1. Question Space: Do you have access to a "Never" account or Health Savings Account (HSA) with a company contribution? *(Note: You will only have access to this account if you are participating in a high deductible health plan.)*

    a. Action Space: Open and fund the account through the financial vendor used by your employer. This first action aligns with what we just talked about which was prioritizing free money! *(Note: If your employer offers a high deductible health plan option, you can typically sign up during the annual enrollment period.)* Now let's move to the next question space.

2. Question Space: Do you have access to a "Later" account (e.g., 401k, 403b) with a company match? *(Note: This is the account we discussed in our example above with the $250,000 increase based on taking advantage of the company match or free money)!*

    a. Action Space: Open and fund the account up to the match. In our example above, the employer was matching 3%, so in that case, you should contribute 3% to receive the full benefit of free money. Now our hunt for free money is over, so let's move to the next priority.

3. Question Space: Are you eligible to contribute to a "Now" account? *(Note: This will be based on your income level or how much you earn and the IRS guidelines. Please review the previous section on "Now" accounts or Google "Roth IRA IRS income limits.")*

    a. Action Space: Open and fund a "Now" account with as much as possible and up to the IRS limit of approximately $6,000. *(Note: As previously mentioned, these limits change periodically so Google "IRS Roth IRA contribution limit" to get the current amount.)*

4. Question Space: Are you willing to save more?

    a. Action Space: Contribute the IRS maximum to your "Later" account from Question Space 2 *(Note: Yes, the limits change periodically and you should use Google to find the current limits!).*

5. Question Space: Are you willing to save more?

    a. Action Space: Open and fund an "Always" account or taxable brokerage account. *(Note: I would recommend using the same companies that were mentioned previously for any individual investment account: Charles Schwab, Vanguard, or Fidelity Investments.)*

Congratulations! We now have learned about the various types of investment accounts and how we should prioritize them to make the most of our limited money to invest. These are huge and complicated steps. Unfortunately, we aren't done! In a perfect world, you've walked through the board game and money is starting to automatically roll into these accounts from your direct deposit, but now that money needs to be invested. Before we begin, let me say that this next step is the most important element of walking to wealth, but it's also the one without a correct answer. Let me explain.

Based on research by Vanguard[iv] as well as others, approximately 90% "of your experience (the volatility you encounter and the returns you earn) can be traced back to your asset allocation." Asset allocation is simply a term to describe how you distribute your money across various investment options. Okay, so now we know why it's important given that it's responsible for 90% of our success, so I should just tell you where to invest or create another board game and we can move on, right? I wish it were that easy!

To start, let's discuss our options, which is the first problem or if you are glass half full, the first opportunity.

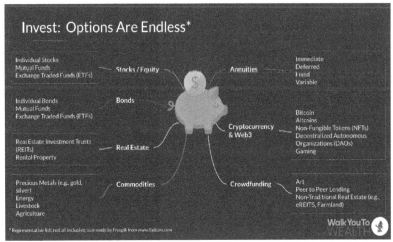

Invest: Options Are Endless*

Individual Stocks
Mutual Funds
Exchange Traded Funds (ETFs) — Stocks / Equity

Annuities — Immediate
Deferred
Fixed
Variable

Individual Bonds
Mutual Funds
Exchange Traded Funds (ETFs) — Bonds

Real Estate Investment Trusts (REITs)
Rental Property — Real Estate

Cryptocurrency & Web3 — Bitcoin
Altcoins
Non-Fungible Tokens (NFTs)
Decentralized Autonomous Organizations (DAOs)
Gaming

Precious Metals (e.g., gold, silver)
Energy
Livestock
Agriculture — Commodities

Crowdfunding — Art
Peer to Peer Lending
Non-Traditional Real Estate (e.g., eREITS, Farmland)

* Representative list; not all inclusive; icon made by Freepik from www.flaticon.com

Walk You To WEALTH

Imagine for a second going to the grocery store to buy a gallon of milk, and when you walk in every shelf is packed with a different variety (almond, cashew, goat, 1%, 2%, chocolate, etc.). The good news is that there is a lot to choose from, the bad news is that there is a lot to choose from. Below is an overview of some of our investment options, which we will review in detail:

Stocks/Equity - Represents ownership in a specific company that has chosen to be publicly available or traded. There are about 40,000 publicly traded companies in the world or 40,000 gallons of milk (overwhelmed yet!). In other words, right now I can log in to my "Always" account and research over 40,000 companies to invest in, including popular names that you likely know, such as Amazon, Netflix, Google, Microsoft, Apple, Disney, and Walmart, plus 39,993 more! Successfully investing in individual stocks requires time, patience, and in my opinion, the most important element is luck. Let's go back to the grocery store analogy for a second. Imagine sifting through all the nutritional information on the back of each gallon of milk to determine the 1 out of 40,000 that you think will be better than the rest. Hopefully you agree that it would be time consuming, and you'd be lucky to have picked the best gallon.

The stock market, meaning all of the publicly listed companies, tends to be highly volatile in the short-term; however, it produces great long-term results. For example, the U.S. stock market has returned an average of approximately 10% over its history; however, it's also declined by almost 50% in a single year! I could now bore you with countless short-term charts and stories about the dot-com bubble, the 2008 recession, or the first quarter of the pandemic in which the market tumbled, but I don't think those will be useful. Instead, the best analogy to the stock market is a healthy long-term relationship. Hopefully, you have had at least one of those in your life and it could be with anyone, a spouse, mother, father, grandparent, sibling, friend, etc., as long as it is healthy and has existed for at least 10 years. If so, take a minute to think about that relationship and now think about any one shorter period of that relationship. It could be a day, a month, or a year. It could be some great high moment or a significant low. This is how healthy relationships generally work, there are periods of great highs and some difficult moments, but overall, and when looked at from the entirety of the 10-plus years, it's healthy, and usually seems like it's been a smooth ride, despite the short-term highs and lows. Maybe you couldn't stand your parents during your teenage years (fingers crossed I avoid this with my two boys when they get there!) or didn't like your college roommate when you first met even though you ultimately became best friends. For me, I've been happily married for 16 years, and over the long-term, this is a healthy and wonderful relationship; however, if you looked at a small window or snapshot on our worst day, month, or quarter during those 16 years, it would likely tell you a different story. One of those periods was when we first had children and moved to the suburbs, which was a hard adjustment for both of us. She was home alone all day with two babies and I was commuting two hours a day for work. During this stretch, like any good long-term relationship, we had some low periods. If you judged our marriage on only those times, or if one of us overreacted and panicked due to them, we would have missed out on all the goodness that was right around the corner. This is the same with the market. You need to understand that it performs well over the long-term, but if you are going to panic and sell when it's having a bad day, month, quarter, or year, then it's not the best place for you to invest.

The stock market is generally broken-down in two ways, size and geography. In terms of size, there are four primary buckets of publicly traded companies:

1. Large-cap: Value of $10 billion and greater

2. Mid-cap: Value of $2 billion to $10 billion

3. Small-cap: Value of $300 million to $2 billion

4. Micro-cap: Value of $50 million to $300 million

In terms of geography, it is generally classified as U.S. or domestic and international markets, which excludes the U.S. The international markets are then further broken-down into "Developed" and "Emerging" markets. Developed markets are those with well-established economies, markets, and governments, such as the U.K., Canada, and Australia, while emerging markets are those that are less developed, such as China, India, and Brazil.

Bonds - Represents a loan to a government or company that will be paid back over a certain period of time with a specified amount of interest. The percentage of interest you earn is directly correlated with the risk of default, or the risk of never getting paid back, and the length of the loan. We've likely all begrudgingly lent money to a friend or family member and knew the ones who were never going to pay us back or who it would take forever to collect from. This is the same idea with bonds. The bigger the risk of default and the longer the length of the loan, the higher the interest rate. For example, short-term (2-year) bonds issued by the U.S. Government may have a 1% interest rate, but if you lent that money to the U.S. Government for a much longer period of time, say 30 years, the interest rate may be approximately 2%. In other words, you can earn double, or 1% more in our example, by agreeing to loan your money for an additional 28 years. So, now you can clearly see how the length of the loan will impact the interest you earn. The other factor is risk of default. If you lent money to a high quality publicly traded company for 30 years, you would likely earn over 3% by comparison to the 2% from the U.S. Government, because there is a higher chance that the company defaults on the loan or never pays you back. As with all investments, this is a risk and reward scenario where the more risk you take the higher the reward. In general, bonds, especially those issued by the federal government, tend to be less volatile than stocks and provide safer, but lower, long-term returns.

Although stocks and bonds vary significantly, there is one common denominator between them which is how they can be purchased. There are three potential options: individually, bundled as part of a mutual fund, or bundled as part of an Exchange Traded Fund (ETF). Buying an individual stock or bond is exactly as it sounds. You are choosing an individual stock, such as Disney, or an individual bond, and deciding that you think this one is better than the others. By comparison, mutual funds and ETFs allow you to buy a collection of stocks and/or bonds. As an example, a stock mutual fund that is concentrated in technology companies would include varying amounts of stock in companies like Google, Apple, and Microsoft. If we return to the grocery store scenario one more time, it's essentially a way to easily purchase different types of milk with a single transaction and by default, a lot less research and risk. ETFs and mutual funds are similar, with the main difference being how quickly you can buy or sell shares. ETFs are traded throughout the trading day, which is 9:30-4:00 (ET) for the U.S. stock market whereas mutual funds are priced and traded only once per day after the stock market closes. In other words, you can buy an ETF at noon on Monday, but if you place an order to purchase a similar mutual fund, it will not be processed until the end of the trading day.

Real Estate - Physical real estate can be a terrific investment, and I am the owner of a rental property that was my first home with my wife. Let me start by saying that we've been lucky landlords. In over ten years, we've had the same tenant who pays on time and never complains. We are also fortunate to have refinanced our mortgage before we moved which locked in a low interest rate and allowed us to breakeven on a monthly basis prior to paying off the mortgage. Additionally, since we started renting, the property has almost doubled in value. Although we've been lucky, real estate can be a fair amount of work, requires a lot of research, and typically requires debt in the form of a mortgage. I don't use the word "lucky" often to describe my investments, but I will here, as anytime you invest a large sum of money in a single asset, whether it be a property or an individual stock, it's more like gambling than investing. For every story like mine, there are countless stories about landlords going to court with their tenants, dealing with months of maintenance issues, and/or long vacancies. Again, real estate can be a great way to build wealth and even today it is responsible for a significant percentage of my net worth, but just know that it requires research into the specific market, actual work from time to time, and an occasional headache. Another potential downside is that physical real estate isn't liquid. Meaning that if I needed or wanted to sell my property it would likely take a significant amount of time, energy, paperwork, and money. By contrast, selling a mutual fund or ETF requires a few clicks, no paperwork or fees, limited taxes and the money is typically available after two business days.

If you like the idea of real estate and owning something that is more tangible, but you don't want to be a landlord, research specific markets, or be concerned about liquidity, then investing in a Real Estate Investment Trust (REIT) may be a great option. There are two main types of REITs, an Equity REIT which generates income through the collection of rent and/or the sale of property, and a Mortgage

REIT which invests and earns income from mortgages. REITs are an excellent way to have exposure to real estate as an investment without having to do any of the maintenance associated with a property. By law, a REIT must pay out at least 90% of its taxable income. In other words, if a REIT earned $100,000 of taxable income, it must pay out $90,000 to its owners, which could be you. As with physical real estate, REITs can include commercial space, such as shopping malls, health care facilities, office space, and hotels, residential real estate, and/or mortgage securities. Similarly, to the stocks and bonds we discussed above, you can purchase an individual REIT or a collection of them in the form of a mutual fund or ETF.

Lastly, you can invest in real estate through various non-traditional avenues, including crowdfunding sites, which we will discuss later in this chapter.

Commodities - You can invest in commodities, such as precious metals, livestock, agriculture, or energy. The easiest way to invest in commodities is through a mutual fund or ETF, which tracks the commodities market. This includes gold, silver, oil, gas, coffee beans, sugar, hogs, cattle, corn, and soybeans. You can invest directly in the commodities market or in publicly traded companies that extract or process the materials. In other words, you can purchase gold as a commodity or shares in a publicly traded gold mining company. Similarly, to stocks and bonds above, you can choose to invest in a broad set of commodities or a single one or individual company.

Annuities - An annuity is typically a long-term investment through an insurance company in which you provide the insurance company with a sum of money, either a lump sum or a series of payments, and in return they provide you with a guaranteed paycheck, typically for life. These are essentially pension plans that you can self-fund. The benefits are primarily emotional and mental, which shouldn't be discounted. For example, multiple studies have shown that retirees with ample guaranteed income were happier in retirement. I'm not retired yet, but I won't dispute these studies as worrying about running out of money is typically the number one concern for most retirees and an annuity can limit or remove that concern. Now for the bad news, these are typically expensive, complicated, and generate investment returns that are much lower than other investments. Again, there is a risk and reward tradeoff, you are buying guaranteed income and peace of mind, but it comes with higher fees and opportunity cost. If you are interested in annuitizing some of your retirement savings, I would recommend waiting until you are closer to retirement and purchasing an immediate annuity. For now, the important takeaway is that annuities are an investment option to create a guaranteed stream of income for life.

Cryptocurrency & Web3 - Cryptocurrency is the most discussed, tweeted, blogged, and controversial personal finance topic. Bitcoin (BTC), created in 2009, is the primary cryptocurrency, followed by Ethereum (ETH), and seemingly countless other alternatives or altcoins (e.g., Dogecoin, Cardano, Solana). If you've never heard of cryptocurrency, in its simplest form it's a decentralized form

69

of digital money. In other words, it's a way for you to hold, send, receive, and spend money without the involvement and typical fees of the traditional banking system and also without relying on government-controlled fiat currencies. A great example of the power of currency decentralization is the Russia and Ukraine war of 2022 in which the Russian currency, the Ruble, dropped to near worthless overnight. It's hard to imagine a world where the U.S. dollar is worthless one morning, but I bet there were lots of Russians who felt the same way prior to the war. There are countless cryptocurrency believers and also those who dismiss it, such as famed investor Warren Buffett who said, "If you buy something like Bitcoin or some cryptocurrency, you don't have anything that is producing anything." Regardless of the strong feelings on this topic, the market capitalization, or value of the entire cryptocurrency market, is approximately $2T as of the time of this book and whether you are a true believer or a strong skeptic, it's hard to ignore it as an investment option, given its size and potential.

There are also countless opportunities within the larger crypto economy and Web3. Web3 is the idea that there will be a new version of the World Wide Web that is based on the same decentralized blockchain technology that supports cryptocurrency. In this new world, traditional companies, such as big tech and finance, could be severely disrupted. For example, imagine a world where instead of Twitter, Facebook, and TikTok, you are using a platform that is managed by you or anyone else in the world. This space is evolving at a rapid pace much like when the internet was first introduced and will likely continue to expand.

Crowdfunding - You can invest in personal loans, art, start-ups, real estate and many other items through crowdfunding sites and apps. Crowdfunding is a way for a group of people to pool their money together to make a large purchase. Each of these offers a unique opportunity to diversify your investments in what is typically a user-friendly manner. Personally, I also find some of them very interesting. For example, the idea of owning a few acres of farmland in the middle of the country without having to actually farm, sounds appealing to me, and through a crowdfunding site, such as AcerTrader, I can do it. In general, the fees are higher than investing in the stock market, which in fairness, is practically free these days, and the investments aren't highly liquid. In other words, if you choose to invest, you shouldn't use money that you will need access to in the near-term as selling these types of investment may take a considerable amount of time or may not be possible at all.

At this point, I've potentially made it worse, more overwhelming, and complicated given the thousands of options above coupled with how critical this decision is. To reiterate, how you allocate your money is responsible for approximately 90% of your potential success, according to the Vanguard study that I cited earlier. Given the importance of this decision, let's see if we can glean some insights from three of the most successful investors of all time. Perhaps, Peter Swensen, Yale's former Chief Investment Officer, Warren Buffett, founder and CEO of Berkshire Hathaway, and Ray Dalio, founder of one of the world's largest hedge funds, Bridgewater Associates, can help us figure out how to allocate our money and find the right gallons of milk!

THERE IS NO RIGHT ANSWER

I was wrong! Turns out that studying some of the greatest investors of our time won't help us find the perfect answer to the most important investment question. How frustrating is that? No wonder people avoid investing! Below is a snapshot of the three portfolios that were recommended by Peter Swensen, Warren Buffett, and Ray Dalio:

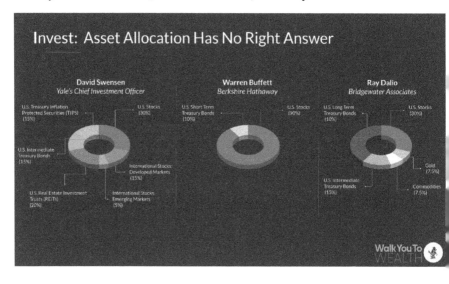

Let's move through each of these from left to right, starting with David Swensen. He recommends 50% of your portfolio be allocated towards stocks, split between U.S. (30%), international developed markets (15%) and emerging markets (5%). Next, David has a 30% allocation to U.S.

Treasury bonds, split evenly between intermediate bonds and inflation protected securities, which return interest based on the rate of inflation. Lastly, he allocates 20% towards REITs, which we discussed earlier.

Next, let's discuss Warren Buffett's recommendation which is the simplest of the three portfolios. Warren recommends a 90% allocation to U.S. stocks and a 10% allocation to short-term U.S. Treasury bonds. In comparison to David Swensen's portfolio, Warren Buffet has a much higher stock allocation, but with no allocation to international stocks. He also doesn't have any REITs which comprised 20% of David Swensen's portfolio. So far, the only alignment seems to be that we need some portion of U.S. stocks, and some form of Treasury bonds. Before we move on from this portfolio, I also want to address a concern you may have about how aggressive Warren's allocation is. We started this chapter with a quote by Mellody Hobson, the chairwoman of Starbucks, who said "The biggest risk of all is not taking one." In other words, Warren's recommendation may be too aggressive for you personally; however, if you flipped this portfolio to 90% short-term bonds and 10% U.S. stocks you would unknowingly be taking a far bigger risk than investing aggressively. Below is an excerpt from a study regarding portfolio success, where "success" is defined as not running out of money over a 30-year period, based on various asset allocations:

Allocation	Success of a 4% Annualized Withdrawal Rate, Adjusted for Inflation, Over 30 Years
100% Stocks	98%
50%/50% Stocks & Bonds	96%
100% Bonds	35%

Select data from Portfolio Success Rates: Where to Draw the Line. The success rate of investment portfolios based on rolling 30-year periods from 1926–2009. Adjusted for inflation.[v]

According to the research, if you were 100% invested in stocks you would have a 98% chance of success or only a 2% chance of running out of money over the course of 30 years; however, if you were 100% invested in bonds you would have a 35% chance of success or a 65% chance of depleting all your funds within the 30 years. This is not to say that you should have a 100% stock portfolio, but rather to demonstrate that Mellody Hobson was absolutely correct and also that Warren's portfolio, while aggressively invested, is still safer than if you were to purely invest in what you may think of as safe assets. If you are wondering how investing 100% in a volatile asset like the stock market can result in lower risk, it simply comes down to the returns. As you start to withdraw funds, especially if you want to keep pace with inflation, or the rising cost of goods and services, it's critical to have some money invested in "riskier" assets, such as the stock market. In other words, over the course of a 30-year period you will likely spend more on living expenses in the later years due to inflation; however, your bond assets may not increase at the same rate, resulting in you withdrawing more money than you are able to earn, and therefore, running out. These are certainly two extremes, but it helps to demonstrate that playing it safe isn't always as safe as you might think it is.

Lastly, we have Ray Dalio who published his portfolio allocation as part of the book Unshakeable by Tony Robbins and Peter Mallouk. Ray recommends a 30% allocation to U.S. stocks, and 25% to U.S. Treasury bonds, which is fairly similar to David Swensen; however, Ray then becomes the first of these three to recommend gold and commodities, with a 7.5% allocation to each. Ray described this as the "All Weather Portfolio," based on the idea that given the diverse allocation it could withstand the test of time through various market cycles.

In summary, all three investors agree that we need anywhere between 30-90% allocated towards U.S. stocks and 10-30% allocated to some form (i.e., long, intermediate, short, inflation protected) of U.S. Treasury bonds. That's not much to go on, but it does confirm one thing, the most important question about investing doesn't have a perfect answer. So, should we give up? Yes and no. Let's give up on trying to find a perfect answer, but let's continue to figure out what may work well for you.

PERSONALITY

75

Knowing yourself and being aware of our natural human biases is a critical step to figuring out how to allocate your money across the various options. In other words, if you are financially conservative by nature, you shouldn't try to invest aggressively, but rather figure out what asset allocation is right for you as an individual. The best way to summarize why this is so important is through tangible evidence. Research performed by Dalbar Inc., [vi] an independent company which analyzed investor returns, concluded that for a 20-year period ending 12/31/2015, the S&P 500 Index (a collection of the 500 largest publicly traded companies in the U.S.) returned an average of approximately 10% a year, while the average equity or stock fund investor earned approximately half that or 5%. How did the average investor in the stock market earn only half of what the market returned? The short answer is by being human. We tend to be impulsive and overreact to both good and especially bad news. There is an entire field, behavioral finance, dedicated to this topic, and below, I will outline some of the key concepts to be aware of:

Loss Aversion: An example of a natural bias is loss aversion which is our tendency to steer clear of losses at all costs, even if the benefits are greater. As a result, we tend to not want to invest at all for fear of losing our hard-earned money.

Herd Mentality: As Mims used to say when I was a kid growing up in New York "If everyone else were jumping off the Brooklyn bridge would you jump too?" In this case, the answer is yes. This impacts our investing because when the stock market, real estate market, or any other market is increasing like crazy, we don't want to miss out on the party, so we jump in as well. Typically, we jump in at the height and then sell later at a low due to a combination of our loss aversion and continuing to follow the herd. Damn you, human brain!

Confirmation Bias: This is a key one given our current use of technology. Ever notice how if you Google something, a good example from my house might be "Spiderman," you start receiving more and more information about Spiderman. To go a step further, if you search "Spiderman, the greatest Avenger," you will start receiving very complimentary articles and information about our friendly neighborhood superhero. This is confirmation bias. We like to surround ourselves with people who agree with us, and in a digital world run by algorithms designed to tell us exactly what we want to hear, this is more prevalent than ever before. In terms of applicability to your investments, try searching for negative stock market predictions such as "market bubble," "bear market," or "stock market collapse," and not surprisingly, nearly every article, Tweet, and message in your feed will confirm the end of the stock market as we know it. Does that mean that it's time to sell before this great crash? Of course not, but we tend to find no shortage of information and "experts" to confirm exactly what we are looking for, whether it's right or wrong.

Why is this so important? It matters because investments, especially riskier ones like stocks, do not earn 10% a year, but rather that is the average with some years being significantly higher and others significantly lower. We've all heard "Buy low and sell high," but in reality, we do the opposite. During times of panic, we have a natural flight or loss aversion mentality, but to be an investor we need to understand ourselves better and learn that the best action during times of market collapse is to do absolutely nothing differently than the day before. Famous investor, Peter Lynch, once said "In the stock market, the most important organ is the stomach. It's not the brain."

Our biases go on and on, but in my opinion, these three are the most impactful to our inability to successfully invest for the long-term. I can't stop us from being human, but you need to be aware of your biases and know that your individual personality should be a substantial driver in determining your investment allocation. If not, you may wind up with half of your potential return (or less – remember that was the average!), as noted earlier.

The point is that you need to know what type of person you are to figure out what type of investor you will be. Next, we will discuss the two most important methods that I've found to counter our natural human tendencies and biases, which are to have a written plan, and to automate your investment process.

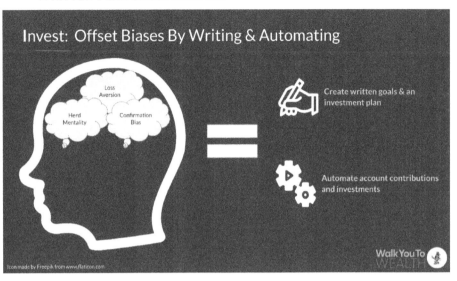

Writing goals has tremendous psychological effects. In a number of studies, written goals and plans have proven to positively impact the likelihood of achieving those goals. This is all about us getting out of our own way! This doesn't need to be a 10-page manifesto, but enough detail on what you want to achieve, why you want to achieve it, and how you are going to get there. Below are my financial goals and information about my plan:

Financial goals:

1. Goal: Support my family's financial needs.

a. **Why?** As I previously mentioned, I've been the only financial support for my family for the last decade while my wife has had the equally, or arguably more important job, of raising our two boys. There is nothing more important to me than knowing my family has everything we need.

2. Goal: Fully fund college for my two boys.

    a. **Why?** College graduates earn approximately 75% more than those with only a high school diploma. Education is expensive, but it's also critical to financial success for most of us who didn't drop out and become the next great tech entrepreneur. I am also open to my children wanting to pursue a trade in lieu of college, but either way, I want them to do it without debt.

3. Goal: Reach financial independence or work optional status by age 47.

    a. **Why?** I love spending time with my family, and I want the ability to spend more time with them without having to think about my next work meeting, email, or trip. I also want to pursue my passion for financial education, but on my own terms. Financial independence for me is about having options, choices, and more time with those I love!

4. Goal: Be debt free by 47.
    a. **Why?** Paying off your home is a surprisingly controversial topic in the world of personal finance, which I will discuss more about later, but for me, I want my home to be paid off by the time I leave my corporate job.

5. Goal: Protect my family financially if anything were to happen to me.
    a. **Why?** If something were to happen to me, I want to know that my family is financially sound. For me, this means investing in term life insurance and also building my "Always" account, so that my wife would have accessible money in the event of my death.

6. Goal: Build a larger emergency fund for retirement.
    a. **Why?** As I get closer to retirement age, I want to expand my cash reserves so that I don't have to worry about money, or more importantly, what the heck is happening to my investments in the short-term.

These are my primary goals. Yours will be different and may include purchasing a home, making your first investment, or opening a "Later" account. They just need to be achievable, measurable, written, and most importantly, include the "why?"

In terms of my investment plan, I document this in two ways: my overall investment philosophy, which is a set of high-level principles about investing, all of which I will cover in detail in this book, and my annual planned contributions to each of my accounts based on my expected income. The first document, my investment philosophy, shouldn't change much over time and helps me from losing focus and getting distracted by the next great investment trend, and the second document helps me project some of these goals and allocate my money, based on the account prioritization that we discussed earlier. I will share my investment philosophy later in this chapter as it summarizes well my personal views on investments and asset allocation. The second document, my annual planned investment contributions, includes a breakdown of investable earned income. Again, I don't budget, but I will figure out how much I can and should invest each year based on my income and projected expenses. In other words, if I earn $100,000 after-tax and generally live-off or spend $65,000 of that to support my lifestyle, I walk through the board game allocation that we previously discussed to determine what accounts will receive my $35,000 of investable money. This would result in fully funding my "Never," "Later," and, "Now" accounts by completing the first three action spaces from our board game. This is key to paying myself first and also not budgeting. At the end of each year, I will see how close I came to my projections which are sometimes impacted by income changes or unexpected expenses throughout the year. This isn't about perfection and being

100% accurate, but rather, a commitment and plan to allocate my money to the most important person, myself.

Again, the most critical step is to write down your goals so that it becomes more likely that you will achieve them. There is magic in writing them down. If you want to go a step further, share them with someone who can hold you accountable (or in my case, publicize them for the world to see).

The second important method to counter human tendencies is to automate your plan. This step will vary in level of complexity depending on where you've chosen to open your investment accounts (e.g., Vanguard, Fidelity Investments) and how your direct deposit is handled at work. For me, I've been fortunate to have fairly intuitive direct deposit systems (i.e., Workday, ADP) that were easy to update and change. This has always been my starting point and the easiest way to pay myself first. I simply choose how my paycheck gets allocated and send money to any number of accounts. Based on the board game steps, I decide my account prioritization and separately how much I am going to contribute based on my investment plan and then I automate the direct deposit step. For a practical example, if I'm going to contribute $6,000 to my "Now" account, or Roth IRA, I will have $250 per check ($6,000/24 pay checks) deposited directly into that account.

The next step is to make sure that the deposits are invested, otherwise I will be sitting on $6,000 of cash 20 years from now instead of approximately $40,000 based on a 10% annual return! So, you need to move to the other side of the automation which is with your investment account provider. You can walk through a few easy clicks to request that your directly deposited funds are automatically invested into mutual funds of your choice at a regular frequency. This will take your human emotions about where the stock or bond market is on any given day out of the conversations in your head. For certain workplace accounts, such as "Never" (HSA) or "Later" (e.g., 401k, 403b) accounts, the account provider (e.g., Charles Schwab, Fidelity Investments, Vanguard) is chosen by your employer and you typically can update the percentage you are willing to contribute through the account provider's site or during your annual benefits enrollment period at work. Similarly, you will then need to automate the investment side on the provider's site, so that your money is actually invested after it is deposited.

As an alternative, you can have all of your money directly deposited into your main checking account and then set up automatic transfers to your non-employer sponsored investment accounts from there; however, I recommend allocating your paycheck directly into multiple accounts as I just described, because you will be less likely to cancel or reverse the automatic transfer and spend the money after it hits your checking account. Below is an image to help illustrate the nuances of the two approaches:

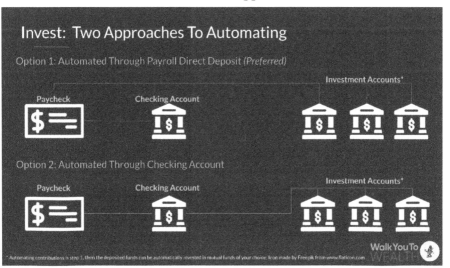

In summary, write and automate. Writing down your goals will help keep you on track and remind you of the "why?" when it's hard to stay focused on the long-term benefits. Secondly, automation will allow you to put the majority of your investments on autopilot so that you can go on living your life while your money starts to work for you. These two steps will be critical to your long-term success, won't take a lot of time to complete, and only need to be reevaluated as infrequently as annually, so that you can make adjustments for raises, promotions, or other life changes.

MY INVESTMENT PHILOSOPHY

Alright, quick recap time. We've completed SIMPLE step 1, to save ourselves from debt and the unexpected and are walking through the complications of step 2, invest. So far, we've discussed how to prioritize investment accounts, the countless investment options, the importance of personality, how to sidestep human tendencies through written goals and automation, and finally, the fact that there is no perfect answer for how to allocate your money to investments. Now, I will discuss my investment philosophy, which I briefly mentioned earlier, as well as my personal asset allocation.

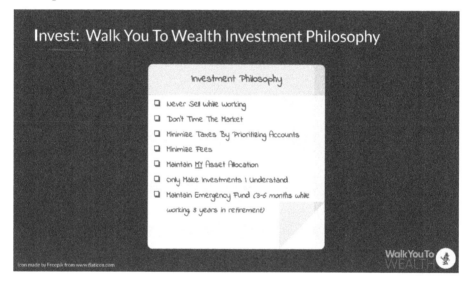

1. Principle - Never Sell While Working: Never sell any investments while working with the exception of rebalancing once per year after annual dividends.

a. **Why?** I am investing for the long-term and selling would likely mean that I am feeding into my fears, premonitions, or natural biases. This rule is important to me and the one that I find the most difficult to stick to, which is another reason why I find it helpful to have it written down. I am as impulsive as the next person, and so, occasionally, I might find something else to invest in, like farmland or cryptocurrency from earlier, but this reminds me not to sell existing investments based on those ideas. In terms of rebalancing, it's a term which simply means bringing your portfolio back to your desired allocation, or back into balance. For example, using Warren Buffett's allocation of 90% U.S. stocks and 10% short-term bonds, if the stock market has outperformed and now comprises 95% of your portfolio, you would sell stocks and buy short-term bonds so that the portfolio is back in balance.

2. Principle - Don't Time The Market: Invest when the cash is available or automatically.

   a. **Why?** You may be concerned about investing in the stock market because you don't want to invest at a high point, or you are nervous about investing as the market is nosediving. To that, I would like to show you an illustration of the stock market that my youngest son drew when he was 5:

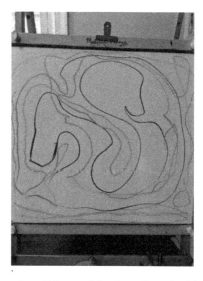

The reason that I love this drawing (aside from the fact that my son drew it), is that he's right! The stock market may drop 20% right after you invest, or it could rise 20%. No one, not even Warren Buffett, or the million stock market prognosticators on CNBC, Twitter, Reddit, or TikTok know what the market is going to do next. That is why it is important to have a written plan and just to start, as opposed to waiting for the "right time," also known as market timing. The right time to invest was yesterday, but the next best time is today!

Additionally, you are statistically better off investing a lump sum in the stock market approximately 70% of the time rather than allocating it throughout the year, otherwise known as dollar-cost-averaging. For example, let's say you have $120 to invest at the start of the year, you are better off investing all $120 on January 1st as opposed to investing

$10/month throughout the year. The reason for this is simply that you could miss the best stock market returns during the days you waited.

So, statistically, you are better off investing lump sums, and if your career is heavily bonus or commission driven, I would do just that. For example, most of my career has been spent in bonus heavy roles and I practice what I preach and invest my lump sum as soon as it is deposited into my investment account (for any investments that aren't automated as part of my regular paycheck). This isn't mentally easy, which is why I automate as much as possible. In May of 2019, I received a bonus that I was planning on investing in the stock market based on my investment plan that I previously mentioned. This period in the market seemed like the beginning of the end based on the pandemic. Specifically, May of 2019 was one of the worst months for the stock market in several years, and seemingly every article and talking head was calling for a pending recession and the market to plummet anywhere from 15% to 50%. The day that my bonus hit my account, I immediately placed the trade as part of my written plan, knowing that in the short-term, according to all the "experts," I may have to watch my investment drop like a rock to the bottom of a lake. I would be lying if I told you it was easy. I would also be lying if I told you that I didn't think about it for months leading up to my bonus, but I kept reminding myself of one thing, NO ONE HAS ANY IDEA WHAT THE MARKET IS GOING TO DO TOMORROW, NEXT WEEK, NEXT MONTH, OR NEXT YEAR. I am also not investing for tomorrow, next week, next month, or next year but rather for 10, 15, or even 30 years from now. In case you are wondering what happened over the next several months, my trade earned approximately 20% through the remainder of the year, just proving that you can't time the market or listen to the "experts." I also know it could have just as likely moved in the opposite direction.

If you still aren't convinced to invest when you have the money, consider this. Based on research from Bank of America, if an investor missed the 10 best stock market days each decade since 1930, their total return would have been approximately 17,000% lower than if they hadn't missed those 10 days. This isn't a typo. A 17,000% difference by missing 10 days each decade, and no one knows when those 10 best days will be. So, unless you have a crystal ball, invest when you can, the moment that you can, so that you aren't missing out on those precious 10 days, whenever they happen! Below is the actual data from the study, and then back to my philosophy:

The difficulties of trying to time the market
Bank of America looked at the impact of missing the market's best and worst days each decade

Decade	Price return	Excluding worst 10 days per decade	Excluding best 10 days per decade	Excluding best/worst 10 days per decade
1930	-42%	39%	-79%	-50%
1940	35%	136%	-14%	51%
1950	257%	425%	167%	293%
1960	54%	107%	14%	54%
1970	17%	59%	-20%	8%
1980	227%	572%	108%	328%
1990	316%	526%	186%	330%
2000	-24%	57%	-62%	-21%
2010	190%	351%	95%	203%
2020	18%	125%	-33%	27%
Since 1930	17,715%	3,793,787%	28%	27,213%

Source: Bank of America, S&P 500 returns

3. Principle - Minimize Taxes by Prioritizing Accounts: Use tax-advantaged or "Never, Now, Later" accounts to minimize taxes.

   a. **Why?** We discussed the importance of taxes earlier. In my opinion, aside from your asset allocation, this is the second most important step to get right. I don't mind paying my fair share of taxes for the schools that my children attend, the paved roads we all take for granted, and countless other government provided amenities in the United States, but I do mind paying more than I need to and you should too.

91

4. Principle - Minimize Fees: Invest primarily in low-cost or free index funds, which for me is where a minimum of 80% of investable money resides.

   a. **Why?** Most investments have costs associated with them. For this section, I will discuss costs associated with investing in the stock and bond markets, as those seem to be the only consistent pieces from our three expert investors we discussed earlier. Let's start with what you are paying for. Mutual funds and ETFs can either be actively or passively managed. For actively managed funds, you pay a premium to have someone else, a professional, decide when and what to buy. In other words, he or she is responsible for choosing the best individual stocks or bonds that make up that mutual fund or ETF. For example, he or she may have done research and realized that Apple stock is undervalued, and therefore, buys more for the fund that you own. This may be a terrific choice if he or she is right; however, there have been several studies that have proven randomly selecting stocks can be just as effective. My best analogy is a grocery delivery service. Let's say you are paying a premium to have a produce expert select your fruit, but then realize that you would be better off having a computer randomly select your apples and oranges, and it's also cheaper. I am generally a firm believer in the old adage "you get what you pay for," but when it comes to investments, it's just not true. These fees will slowly eat away at your returns with minimal, if any, benefit. Before we go through a quick example, let me get something off my chest. My biggest pet peeve with the financial services industry is how these fees are disclosed and paid for. When you purchase a mutual fund or ETF there is an expense ratio associated with it, such as .75% for an actively managed fund or .05% for a passively managed fund. When was the last time you went shopping at Target or Walmart and saw a fractional percentage for a price? It's almost like they are going out of their way to make this as complicated as possible! In order to calculate the cost, you need to take your investment, let's say $1,000 and multiply it by the expense ratio, we'll use the .75% to come up with $7.50/per year. On top of being a fractional percentage, you will never receive a bill for $7.50, rather they will simply take it out of your investment without you ever seeing it. Talk about unintentional spending! Okay, now that I got that off my chest, I feel better, and we can move back to minimizing fees.

By comparison to actively managed funds, passively managed funds are cheaper, tied to an index, and are typically weighted by some agreed upon factor, such as market capitalization. This is just a fancy word for the value of companies. In other words, when Apple became one of the most valuable companies in the United States and was included in the Standard and Poor's 500 Index (S&P 500), an index of the 500 largest companies in the U.S., your S&P 500 mutual fund or ETF automatically purchased Apple to mirror the underlying S&P 500. These passively managed funds have a predefined grocery list, based on the index which they mirror, which makes them cheaper to own. I only invest in stocks and bonds through passively managed index funds. Later, I will discuss and provide specific funds that you can invest in, including the funds that I use, but for now, the key point is that paying a premium for a professional to potentially select a rotten apple or orange isn't worth it, so stick with passively managed index funds. Let me prove the point with a hypothetical example using the same two fees from above, .75% for an actively managed fund and .05% for a passively managed fund. Based on an annual contribution of $10,000 with a 10% return, you would have $201,000 more after 30 years if you invested in the cheaper passively managed fund, and that's assuming that both funds have equal returns, and as we just discussed, passively managed funds tend to outperform their actively managed peers.

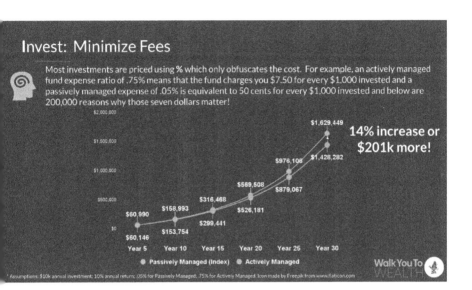

Invest: Minimize Fees

Most investments are priced using % which only obfuscates the cost. For example, an actively managed fund expense ratio of .75% means that the fund charges you $7.50 for every $1,000 invested and a passively managed expense of .05% is equivalent to 50 cents for every $1,000 invested and below are 200,000 reasons why those seven dollars matter!

This cannot be overstated! This isn't my opinion, but rather, a fact and even professional investors, such as the three we discussed earlier, agree that the average investor like you and me, should invest in low-cost or free index funds. The only people who don't agree are the portfolio managers who run actively managed funds and earn millions of dollars each year for minimal performance.

5. Principle - Maintain MY asset allocation: This is a personal choice, but the important piece is to remind myself to stick with it for the long-term.

   a. **Why?** I will discuss my asset allocation in more detail shortly, but the key to this principle is to always maintain my asset allocation plan and rebalance annually.

6. Principle - Only Make Investments I Understand: At my eight-year-old son's physical, his pediatrician was quizzing him about stranger danger. The pediatrician, who seemed more like a great trial lawyer, ended his cross-examination victoriously as my son finally fell prey to the tenth version of the same question by responding "of course" he would help this imaginary stranger find his cat. In fairness to my son, he loves cats, and also confessed later that he just wanted to put an end to the barrage of questions! Following his open court confession, I was deposed on the topic, and we were finally released with a warning. So, how does my son's cross-examination have anything to do with understanding your investments? As we discussed earlier, the world is filled with countless investment opportunities, some of which are relatively straightforward and others that are highly complex and potentially dangerous for average investors. I thoroughly enjoy learning about new and interesting opportunities, but I also only want to invest in something that I understand. This doesn't mean that I need to be an expert, but rather have a fundamental knowledge of the investment objective, underlying technology, how it fits into my overall goals and allocation, the fees, risks, and potential return. In other words, avoid investment stranger danger!

a. **Why?** I will always be interested in investing and new options, so I reserve 10% of my investable assets for alternative investments, to experiment. This is money that I'm willing to potentially lose. I use the word experiment, because some of these may not be true "investments," but rather, a way for me to learn more about a particular investment option. I also enjoy investing, so this allows me to satiate my curiosity without risking the bulk of my assets which are sitting in cheap, reliable, and boring index funds.

7. Principle - Maintain Emergency Fund: Consistently maintain an emergency fund of three months of essential expenses while working and build a cash position of three years' worth for my retirement years.

a. **Why?** While I'm working, I want to ensure I have money set aside for emergencies, but of equal importance is to make good use of my money by investing the majority of it, which is why I only keep three months of essential expenses in my emergency fund. Prior to retirement, I will build this emergency savings to three years' worth of expenses designed to weather any significant downturn in the markets.

My Asset Allocation

As you well know by now, asset allocation is the most important decision to the success of your investments, and below, I will show you my personal asset allocation model and discuss how you should think about yours:

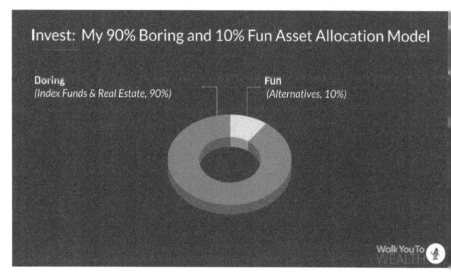

Invest: My 90% Boring and 10% Fun Asset Allocation Model

Boring
(Index Funds & Real Estate, 90%)

Fun
(Alternatives, 10%)

Walk You To WEALTH

My 90% boring and 10% fun asset allocation model is invested primarily in index funds and real estate, with 10% reserved for alternative or "fun" investments. The boring 90% is allocated with 70% to stocks, 10% to bonds, and 10% to real estate, which leaves 10% for fun. Let's discuss each component of my allocation along with the specific funds and investments that are included in my portfolio.

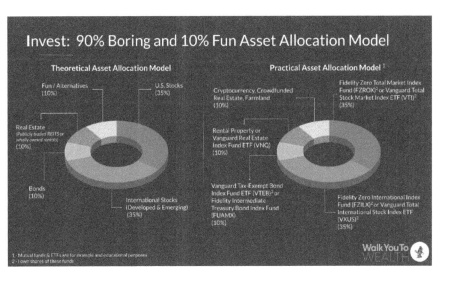

Invest: 90% Boring and 10% Fun Asset Allocation Model

U.S. Stocks: As we discussed earlier, one of the consistencies between the three investment portfolios of Peter Swensen, Warren Buffett, and Ray Dalio was an allocation to U.S. stocks. In my portfolio, I allocate 70% towards stocks, half of which is invested in a total U.S. stock market fund, which is designed to represent the entire U.S. stock market. I generally use the Fidelity Zero Total Market Index Fund (FZROX) for my tax-advantaged accounts and the Vanguard Total Stock Market ETF (VTI) for my "Always" or brokerage account. The Fidelity ZERO Total Market Index Fund (FZROX) is a mutual fund of approximately 2,900 domestic publicly traded companies and costs nothing if your account is at Fidelity. It is literally free! I also own the Vanguard Total Stock Market ETF (VTI), which includes approximately 4,100 domestic publicly traded companies and costs .03% or in plain English 30 cents per year for every $1,000 invested. ETFs are slightly more tax efficient and also pay dividends more frequently than mutual funds, quarterly instead of annually, which are two reasons that I prefer ETFs in my "Always" account despite the slight cost compared to the free Fidelity mutual fund. I will discuss dividends in the next chapter, so don't worry if it's a foreign concept for now. Another option that is similar to VTI is iShares Core S&P Total U.S. Stock Market ETF (ITOT). The list can go on with dozens more, but these are three similar options, and two, that I am personally invested in, covering the U.S. stock market at low or no cost.

International Stocks: As much as I respect Warren Buffett and Ray Dalio, I believe, much like Peter Swensen, that a portfolio with international exposure will help lower your overall risk by increasing your diversification, a fancy way of saying that you own a wider array of companies in varying geographic locations. Most investors tend to favor their hometown or in my case the U.S., much like Warren Buffet, and either skip or undervalue the rest of the world. Specifically, it's estimated that investors in the U.S. have 80-90% of their stock exposure in U.S. companies; however, below are two reasons that I split my stock allocation evenly between the U.S. and the rest of the world:

1) Historically speaking the U.S. and international markets tend to move in inverse cycles over long periods of time. In other words, the U.S. may outperform the international markets for a given 5-, 10-, or 15-year period followed by

the reverse. This helps smooth out some of the bumps within a volatile stock market because when one market is in a long-term down cycle, the other may be enjoying generous and outsized returns. For an extreme example, the Japanese stock market crashed in the early 90s, and still hasn't fully recovered to its previous high in 1989. Think about if you invested 100% in the Japanese stock market, and 30 years later, you still have less money than you started with! Refer to the image below from Morningstar for an illustration of these swings in performance which shows international stock performance relative to the U.S. for 5-year periods since 1975 through 2019:

viii

International vs. U.S. Stocks: 5-Year Rolling Return Gaps

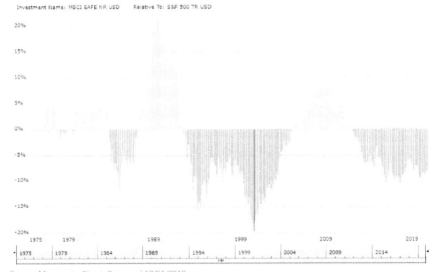

Source: Morningstar Direct. Data as of 10/31/2019

2) Now, if you want to include some percentage of international holdings in your accounts, how much? First, there is no wrong or perfectly right amount, but I allocate half of my stock allocation to international stocks with a very basic line of reasoning. The market capitalization, or total value, of publicly traded companies in the U.S. represents approximately 46% of the total world market value. In other words, the publicly traded companies based in the U.S. represent 46% of all publicly traded companies in the world. Meaning that if you exclude international stocks, you are missing out on 54% of the publicly traded companies in the world. To make my life easier and knowing that there is no wrong or right answer, I simply split it 50/50 instead of shooting for a 46/54 allocation to match the world market capitalization.

In terms of the specific international funds that I own, you will notice a similar pattern to the U.S. funds with similar rationale. I own the Fidelity ZERO International Index Fund (FZILX) which is a mutual fund of approximately 2,500 international and publicly traded companies, and once again, it is completely free if your account is at Fidelity. This fund includes both developed and emerging international markets. As I previously mentioned, developed markets will include countries such as Canada, Australia, and France while emerging markets will be countries such as China, Argentina, and Brazil. Emerging markets tend to be riskier investments with the potential for more growth or return on your money. I also own the

Vanguard Total International Stock Index Fund ETF (VXUS) which has a .07% (70 cents per $1,000 invested) expense ratio and it includes approximately 7,900 public companies across both the developed and emerging international markets. My rationale for owning the Vanguard ETF is the same as above regarding the slight tax advantage and dividend payment frequency for my "Always" account. Similarly, there are other terrific options in this space, including iShares Core MSCI Total International Stock ETF (IXUS) which costs .07% (70 cents per $1,000 invested) and holds approximately 4,300 companies.

Once again, these are only three examples to help make it easier. One word of caution, there are lots of index funds with the word "Total" in the title, but you should read the investment objective and check the composition of the fund to see the geographic dispersion. There are some international index funds that will exclude emerging markets for example, and there are other Total World funds that will include the U.S. and international together. At the end of the day, I want to ensure that I'm covering the U.S., developed international markets, and emerging markets; however, fund names can occasionally be confusing, but all sites will have an easy to read objective and geographic dispersion of the holdings for you to quickly review.

Bonds: As we discussed earlier, bonds will generally lower the risk of your portfolio with also a lower return. Their safety will be driven by the maturity, or the length of time until the loan needs to be paid back, and the quality of the issuer of the bond, with short-term U.S. Treasury bonds being one of the safest investments given that they are guaranteed by the federal government and have a short maturity. The good news first. Bonds are also available in low-cost index funds which should be your primary choice. In terms of percentage allocation to bonds and which bond index funds to purchase, that's up to you. Historically, I've followed Warren Buffet's advice on this and allocated 10% towards my bond index fund; however, to further simplify my life, I hold the entire 10% in one account, my "Always" account. Beyond the simplicity of holding my bonds in one account, I hold them in my "Always" account given my plans for early financial independence. Specifically, I won't be able to access most of my tax-advantaged funds due to the various age restrictions associated with those accounts, but money in my "Always" account will be readily available in the event of a stock market downturn during these early years. You generally don't want to hold bonds or REITs in an "Always" or taxable account, because all the interest earned will be taxed at your ordinary income tax level. In other words, if you are in a 30% income tax bracket all the interest will be taxed at that level. As a result, once I decided to simplify and move my bond allocation to my "Always" account, I decided to change my bond investment to municipal bonds. Municipal bonds are simply loans to state and local entities, with the primary advantage being that the interest the bonds pay is excluded from federal taxes (and also state tax if you own bonds from the state in which you live). I now have my 10% bond allocation in the Vanguard Tax-Exempt Bond Index Fund ETF (VTEB), which has a .06% (60 cents for every $1,000 invested) expense ratio. I could have also handled the simplification in the other direction and held my 10% allocation in my "Never, Now, or Later" account. If I would have gone in that direction, I would have opted for a U.S. Treasury Intermediate bond index fund, such as the Fidelity Intermediate Treasury Bond Index Fund (FUAMX) or the Vanguard Intermediate Term Treasury Index ETF (VGIT), as I would no longer be concerned about the interest being taxed. In summary, bonds pay taxable interest so you want to ensure that you are either holding them in a "Never, Later, or Now" account or if you choose to hold bonds in an "Always" account, then they should be municipal bonds, which will save you significantly on taxes. We will discuss more about interest, dividends, and taxes later, but for now, just know that a percentage of investable assets in bonds generally decreases the volatility of your overall portfolio and provides some safety during prolonged stock market downturns.

Real Estate – This 10% allocation is less than Peter Swensen's recommended 20% and in my personal situation it's in the form of physical real estate as opposed to REITs, both of which we will discuss. Let's start with physical real estate. When I talk about physical real estate as an investment, I mean a rental property that you own directly. For example, I previously mentioned that we purchased a condominium in Boston and after we had kids and moved out of the city, we decided to keep our condo as a rental property. Let me start by repeating that we've been lucky landlords, and as you know by now, I don't use that word lightly. In over ten years, we've had the same tenant who pays on time, never complains, and uses our place more like a hotel than a full residence. He's in his mid-70s, owns multiple homes, and rents our place because he simply doesn't want to commute to work anymore. For every situation like mine, there are others with calls in the middle of the night about leaky faucets, fire alarms, or missing keys and locked doors. There are also properties which have experienced a significant decrease in value or years without being able to find a suitable tenant. This doesn't mean that rental properties aren't a good investment, and a potentially great way to build wealth, just know that it requires research into the specific market, actual work, and an occasional headache. If you choose to enter this world, you should go in with eyes wide open and with reasonable expectations. As much as I like rental properties, I've never had to replace the roof on my index fund, like I had to on my condo's building a few years ago for about $20,000. Again, this doesn't mean that physical real estate is a poor investment option, just know that there are real, and sometimes, immediate expenses involved. Physical real estate is also not liquid as we discussed earlier.

If you like the idea of real estate and owning something that is more tangible, but you don't want to deal with the actual work, research, or liquidity concerns, then investing in a REIT may be a great option. These are also available in the form of low-cost index funds, such as the examples below:

–   Fidelity MSCI Real Estate Index (FREL): This fund holds approximately 175 publicly traded REITs within the United States, with a .08% expense ratio (80 cents for every $1,000 invested).

- iShares Core U.S. REIT ETF (USRT): This fund holds approximately 150 publicly traded REITs within the United States, with a .08% expense ratio (80 cents for every $1,000 invested).

- Vanguard Real Estate ETF (VNQ): This fund holds approximately 170 publicly traded REITs within the United States, with a .12% expense ratio ($1.20 for every $1,000 invested).

As previously mentioned, by law, a REIT must pay out at least 90% of its taxable income. From a tax perspective, you generally want to invest in REITs through a "Never, Now, or Later" account, due to the fact that these payments are taxed at ordinary income tax levels, which we will discuss more, later. Also, much like the individual stocks, you can purchase individual REITs, but the same logic around individual stock risk and research applies.

There are also a number of crowdfunded and non-traditional real estate investment options available; however, this 10% is reserved for wholly owned rental property or publicly traded REITs, preferably in the form of low-cost index funds.

Alternatives: This is the 10% that I allocate to fun and trying new ideas. This money will be allocated towards smaller investments that are new or interesting, such as cryptocurrency and crowdfunded farmland. That being said, it should be reserved for whatever interests you. The point is to have some money where you can try new investments and learn without risking the bulk of your portfolio. My 10% is currently allocated to various cryptocurrencies, and I'm planning to invest through crowdfunding sites, including AcreTrader, which allows you to invest in farmland across the country. I am also very interested in music and movie royalties, fine art, peer-to-peer lending, small businesses, and countless other investments; however, I haven't yet pulled the trigger on any others yet. We live in a time when investment options are almost limitless, which is great, but you need to be disciplined, so as not to risk more of your portfolio than you can afford on these alternatives, which is why I limit my exposure to 10%. If you are more conservative or less interested in investing, you could allocate nothing to this portion of your portfolio or limit it to 5%. I cannot reiterate enough that there is no perfect or right answer to asset allocation, but 10% allows me to satiate my curiosity for investing and have some fun without risking the bulk of my investments.

In summary, I maintain a fairly simple portfolio which is 90% boring and 10% fun. It's primarily invested in index funds that cost pennies and provide investment returns across the U.S. stock, international stock, and municipal bond markets. This is the power and value of index funds. I also allocate 10% to real estate and 10% to fun alternatives which allows me a guilt free way to experiment and learn. Lastly, all the funds that I mentioned above have low or no minimums to invest. I've invested cents at times, because as you know, I invest the second that my money is available, as little as it may be!

PAY MORE AND DO LESS

If the above portfolio allocation seemed overwhelming, then the bad news is that I'm not doing a very good job, but the good news is that there are two more even simpler options. For a slight premium, you can invest in what's known as a target date fund, and for an even higher premium, you can use a robo-advisor. These are two simple ways that have been developed by financial services companies to allocate investments based on a specific date or goal. A target date fund uses a date, such as your expected retirement, and becomes more conservative as that date approaches. In other words, if I'm retiring in 2040, and I invest in a Target Date 2040 fund, it will slowly reallocate itself and become more conservative with less stock exposure and more bonds as I approach 2040. This is an easy way to set it and truly forget it, but it comes with a slightly higher cost, and the loss of freedom to choose how aggressively or conservatively you want to invest as it's determined by the company who manages the fund, such as Vanguard or Fidelity. If you decide that a target date fund seems like a good option, just make sure that it's an index-based fund. For example, the Fidelity Freedom 2040 Fund is actively managed and has an expense ratio of .75% ($7.50 per $1,000 invested) while the passively managed Fidelity Freedom Index 2040 Fund has an expense ratio of .12% ($1.20 per $1,000 invested). My preference is always passively managed and cheaper investments. If you want something simple, reasonably priced, and which doesn't even require you to rebalance annually or adjust your portfolio over time, then target date index funds are a good option.

A robo-advisor is similar to the target date fund; in that it auto-rebalances based on a set of priorities. The main difference is that it can be customized for you, as opposed to being set by the fund company. There is no shortage of robo-advisor options, and similar to what I said about target date funds, if you want simple and are willing to pay a premium, it's another option, but given the fees it's not one that I would choose.

My hope is that by the end of this book, you feel comfortable enough to develop your own portfolio, but if not, these are two other alternatives, and one, target date index funds, that I recommend.

In summary, investing can be simplified to a one-fund target date portfolio, a two-fund portfolio like Warren Buffett, or a 90% boring and 10% fun portfolio like me, and personality is a significant piece of this puzzle. For example, I will always be a more aggressive investor and don't foresee a point in my life where I will ever hold more than 10% of bonds in my portfolio. Below is a quick illustration of three retirement allocations that may help to bring together some of our conversation around personality and time driving your asset allocation:

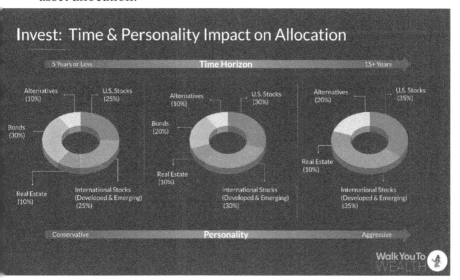

The illustration assumes that you may need to start drawing down or using the money from the portfolio over a period of time, such as retirement, but not that you would need or use the entire balance at a set time. If you need the entire balance of your portfolio for a specific purpose, such as a home purchase or college tuition, within one to five years, then that money is savings and not investments and should be safely sitting in an FDIC insured account or short-term treasury bonds.

SIMPLE STEP 2 – SUMMARY OF ACTIONS (OWN)

We covered a lot during this part of our walk, so let's summarize our actions for the second SIMPLE step, Invest, on our walk to wealth, which will help you OWN your future:

- **O**pen accounts based on the prioritization – Open the necessary accounts in priority order to ensure that you are taking advantage of free money followed by tax-advantaged accounts.

- **W**rite down goals and automate your investment plan – Figure out and write down your goals and investment plan. Set up automatic contributions to your investment accounts through your payroll provider, or through automatic transfers from your checking account, and then set up automatic investments into low or no cost index funds for the majority of your investable money.

- **N**o right answer for asset allocation – Understand that asset allocation is the most important investment question without a right answer. Take the time to figure out the right allocation for you based on your personality and goals. Choose an allocation that you can stick with through volatile market cycles as actively trading, or changing your mind based on the noise of the market, will likely result in significant losses. Rebalance annually or pay a slight premium for a target date index fund.

CHAPTER THREE: SIMPLE STEP 3 – MONEY BABIES

"Money is a terrible master but an excellent servant."

P.T. Barnum

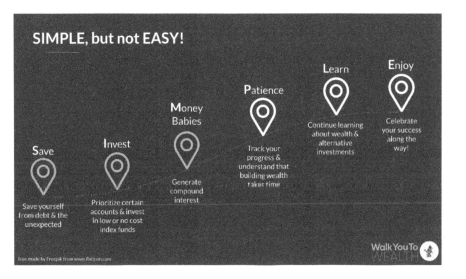

When my children were 5 and 7, I wanted them to invest part of their allowance and I had to figure out a way to explain to them the concept of interest, and more importantly, compound interest. My explanation was two words: "Money babies." The story that I told them was a ridiculous tale about a dollar who gave birth to a penny, dime, and nickel, who in turn, gave birth to more children, grandchildren, great grandchildren, and so on (hopefully, you get the point!). This concept of "money babies," or, more commonly known as compound interest, is the most critical reason to invest and how most wealth is created. Compound interest varies significantly from simple interest. Simple interest is paid out and not reinvested. For example, if you invested $10,000 and earned 10% interest, you would earn $1,000 per year. Not bad! After five years of investing, you would have a total of $15,000 from your initial investment of $10,000; however, if that $1,000 of annual interest were reinvested and you earned interest on that interest, you would have a total of $16,105 after five years. At this point, you might be thinking why are we wasting time talking about earning an extra $1,105 over five years or $221

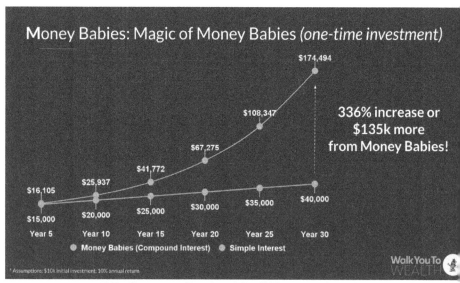

Money Babies: Magic of Money Babies *(one-time investment)*

336% increase or $135k more from Money Babies!

$174,494
$108,347
$67,275
$41,772
$25,937
$16,105
$15,000 $20,000 $25,000 $30,000 $35,000 $40,000

Year 5   Year 10   Year 15   Year 20   Year 25   Year 30

● Money Babies (Compound Interest) ● Simple Interest

*Assumptions: $10k initial investment; 10% annual return

per year? Before you dismiss this difference, let's look at this same example, but extend the time frame to 30 years:

114

Over 30 years, the magic of money babies could earn you 336% or $135,000 more! This is precisely why the best day to invest was yesterday, and the second-best day is today! Next, let's talk about how these money babies are born.

Dividends: The primary source of money babies is dividends. Dividends are a distribution of a company's profits. In other words, if you are invested in a broad range of publicly traded companies through your stock index fund, some of those companies will pay dividends. Let's take a quick detour here to answer two questions that come up often: why don't all publicly traded companies pay dividends? And why would I want to own shares of a company that doesn't pay dividends? These are both great questions.

Companies will ultimately decide if they choose to pay dividends. It's not that some companies are generous, and others aren't, but rather, some companies feel they can better use that money by investing it back in the company through new products, services, acquisitions, or employees. Which brings us to the next question, why would you want to own a company that doesn't pay dividends? Simple; sometimes the companies that reinvest their money make the right choice and those investments pay significantly more than a dividend. For example, the best performing individual stock from 2010-2020 was Netflix with a return of approximately 4,000% (and yes, you read that correctly!). This doesn't mean you should buy Netflix stock, but rather, that some of the best performing companies, such as Netflix, don't pay dividends, which is why you want to invest in a broad mix of companies through an index fund.

Now, back to dividends. The dividend rate of the U.S. stock market has been approximately 2% over the last few years, which when taken with price appreciation, has historically averaged approximately 10% in total stock market returns. By comparison, the international market dividend rate has been approximately 3%. If you hold index funds in your "Always" or taxable account, these will be taxed when received, typically quarterly for ETFs, and annually for mutual funds, and generally at the dividend tax rate, which, historically, has been lower than your income tax rate, including 0% if your income is below $41,675 (filing single) or $83,350 (filing married) for 2022. This special dividend tax rate only applies if; 1) the dividends are "Qualified," and 2) the stock index fund is held in an "Always" or taxable account. In other words, there are no tax implications for dividends in "Never, Now, Later" accounts, which is a primary reason why we prioritized those accounts. In terms of being "Qualified," the IRS classifies dividends as ordinary or qualified. The key item of note is that most publicly traded companies in the U.S. pay qualified dividends, and therefore, qualify for the lower tax treatment, with the primary exception being REITs.

REITs: As I mentioned earlier, REITs are required to pay out 90% of their profits annually to shareholders, which is great! This has resulted in an approximate 3% dividend payment in recent years; however, these are treated as ordinary dividends and are therefore taxed at your ordinary income bracket level. This matters! Let's take the situation of someone who earns less than $40,000, and therefore, would be paying 0% on qualified U.S. stock dividends in 2022, that same person would be paying 12% in taxes on these dividends from REITs. Does that mean that REITs are terrible investments? No. It simply means that if you choose to allocate money to REITs, similar to Peter Swensen's portfolio, they should ideally be held in "Never, Now, Later," or tax-advantaged accounts, similar to our earlier conversation about most bond investments.

Bonds: Speaking of bonds, as we discussed earlier, bonds are simply loans that pay interest or money babies in return for your loan. This interest is taxed as ordinary income, which similar to REITs, means that they should be held in tax-advantaged accounts. The one exception that I discussed as part of my allocation are municipal bonds. These still pay interest; however, they are tax-free at the federal level, and at the state level, if the bonds are issued from the state where you reside. For example, I live in Massachusetts, and so, if I invest in Massachusetts municipal bonds, I will pay no tax at the federal or state level on the interest. Some states also don't have income tax, such as Florida and New Hampshire, so that second benefit would be irrelevant, but the key is not needing to pay federal taxes on the interest.

As I mentioned earlier, you can choose to have your dividends and interest from your index funds paid in cash or reinvested. Fortunately, they are defaulted to be reinvested so that your money babies can continue to expand their family for generations, but at a certain point when you want or need to receive that money they can be set to be paid in cash to either help build up your emergency fund for retirement as I plan to do, or to create a quarterly paycheck without the need to sell any investments.

As you saw from the chart above, the magic of money babies takes time, which we will discuss next, but first some action steps.

SIMPLE STEP 3 – SUMMARY OF ACTIONS (MAGIC)

Let's summarize our actions for the third SIMPLE step, Money Babies, on our walk to wealth, which have been described by Einstein as the "8th wonder of the world," or what I describe as MAGIC:

- **M**oney Babies – Understand the magic of compound interest, or as it's known in my house; Money Babies.

- **A**llocate assets thoughtfully by account type – Money babies come in various forms (e.g., qualified dividends, ordinary dividends, interest) with varying tax consequences, so you want to be thoughtful about what investments (e.g., REITs, bonds) you are holding in which accounts.

- **G**ains over time – The earlier you start to create your

118

family of money babies, the larger your family will grow.

- Imagine – Imagine a world where your money works harder than you do! Money babies are how to create that world!

- Check your automatic reinvestment – Check to make sure that your investments are set to automatically reinvest any dividends or interest payments. This is typically the default setting, but worth checking so that you aren't earning simple interest.

CHAPTER FOUR: SIMPLE STEP 4 – PATIENCE

"The Stock Market is designed to transfer money from the Active to the Patient."

Warren Buffett

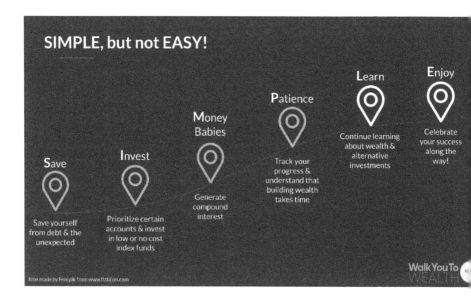

When I was 22 and just finished my MBA, I started to get interested in golf. I picked up a few golf magazines one day and after the sections on swing mechanics and the best clubs to buy, they had information on golf real estate. I grew up in Queens, New York, so the idea of golf real estate was a foreign concept. I knew what golf was and what real estate was, but never imagined that people lived on golf courses. Another reason why I was fascinated by this section, which anyone living on the east or west coast can greatly appreciate, were the prices! I couldn't believe that you could buy a home on a golf course for less than a parking space in New York. One of the areas that was advertised the most was Myrtle Beach, South Carolina. I had never been to either of the Carolinas but convinced my dad to go on a trip with me to Myrtle Beach after I graduated to potentially buy a golf condo. Please bear in mind that this trip is planned in May, right after I'm about to graduate with my MBA and move back home with my parents. In case you doubted how amazing my parents were, imagine supporting the idea of your child buying a golf condo in a different state, right after you helped pack up his college belongings and moved him back into your house!

We flew out of New York on a warm morning in late May, and armed with about $10,000 from internship savings, and a signing bonus from the job that I had lined up for September, I went shopping for a golf condo with my dad. We looked at about a dozen places, including oceanfront condos. You can imagine how my head was now exploding at the idea of being able to choose between overlooking the 18th fairway or the ocean! After three days of hanging out with my dad, I purchased a two-bedroom golf condo at the Barefoot Resort for approximately $125,000. Let's stop for one second so that I can reiterate the insanity of this situation. I had just purchased my first home, a rental property hundreds of miles away, and would be sleeping in my childhood bedroom when the plane landed back in New York. I still remember celebrating with my dad in Myrtle Beach and him commenting that most people would just talk about doing something like this, but very few ever actually have the courage to do it.

I later visited the condo with Mims once it was fully furnished (on a side note, because I was going to rent it, I bought a furniture package that included everything from couches to coffee cups without ever needing to visit a store or unpack a box!). We also visited with my entire family, including my now wife and then girlfriend, who must have been questioning my sanity. I had no plan and knew nothing about real estate investing, but here I was with a golf condo in South Carolina while I lived at home with my amazing parents in New York.

Flash forward; I rented the condo for a few years, which was all taken care of by the resort itself for a fee (hard to imagine, but this was pre-Airbnb), and I eventually sold it when I moved out of my parent's house and got married. I was lucky, and again, I don't use that word often to describe my financial achievements, that the real estate market had increased significantly in those few years. The profit from the condo sale, along with our savings, was used to purchase the first home I was actually going to live in, my condominium in Boston.

My point is not to recklessly throw money around at random ideas from magazines (or in today's world, Twitter, Reddit, Instagram, or TikTok) and hope for high returns. My point is that my dad was 100% right. There are times when you just need to act, to start, to do something. This is why starting, whether it's with $1, $10, or $100 is the most important step. As I said earlier, this walk isn't about getting rich quickly, but the sooner that you start the more time you will have for multiple generations of money babies to be born. Some people will read this and say, but I'm already 40 or 50 or 60, why start now? As I've said repeatedly, yesterday would have been a better day to start, but starting today is still infinitely better than waiting until tomorrow. The hardest part of walking to wealth is being patient enough to get there, especially when there are so many distractions along the way. Next, we will discuss two of the biggest distractions in our world today.

DELAYED GRATIFICATION & LIFESTYLE INFLATION

Part of being patient is delayed gratification and avoiding lifestyle inflation by not keeping up with the Joneses. Let's start with delayed gratification. The legendary marshmallow experiment from Stanford University is likely the most referenced test on this topic. If you aren't familiar with it by some odd chance, you essentially give a child a marshmallow and promise him or her a second marshmallow if they don't gobble the first one down within a certain amount of time. Inevitably some kids enjoy their first and only marshmallow, and who can blame them, while others choose to wait until they can earn a second one. It's this delayed gratification that's increasingly harder in our current world where seemingly all gratification is instant.

Think about our world today and all the amazing conveniences. I can order food, groceries, clothes, or just about anything else and they are delivered within minutes or hours. My home office faces the street and every day, usually multiple times a day, I see the Amazon van as a continuous symbol of the death of delayed gratification. In true fashion of never being hypocritical, I am a frequent Amazon customer and am therefore baffled when I place an online order from somewhere else and it takes more than a few hours to arrive! Amazon and other companies know that delayed gratification is a weakness of all people, including me. This is why trying to delay our gratification is most often a futile effort. So, should we give up and just click "Buy Now" on that new pair of boots? Of course not! The answer lies in what we already discussed way back at the beginning of our walk, the idea of spending intentionally. If you are spending your money intentionally, delayed gratification becomes irrelevant. In other words, if you are choosing to spend your money on that pair of boots, by all means you should get them as soon as possible. The sacrifice comes in eliminating the unintentional spending that we already discussed.

Now, onto the more difficult topic of lifestyle inflation. I live in an affluent area, and it would be easy for me to look around at the bigger homes, swimming pools, and luxury cars (in three and four car garages!) and want all those things that my neighbors have. This has been a problem since the dawn of time. There is a great quote about this by Teddy Roosevelt who said, "Comparison is the thief of joy." In today's world, this problem is immensely magnified since the days of Teddy Roosevelt. Thanks to social media, you are not only comparing yourself with your physical neighbors, friends, and colleagues, but also online connections, celebrities, and athletes from around the world. Let's be honest, social media is mainly a place for bragging or complaining and it's the bragging that drives us to try and keep up with the Joneses. This is one of the few areas that I'm not guilty of and doesn't impact me personally, but it's also one where I don't have many good recommendations. I generally avoid social media, which I know many people would find impossible. I also have the type of confidence and personality that doesn't care much about what others think of me, outside of my wife, kids, and parents. That being said, I realize that staying off social media or raising your sense of indifference to what people think are fairly impractical tips for most people, but let me try anyway. According to multiple studies, we average approximately 2.5 hours per day on social media. This means that over the course of an 80-year life you will spend about 64,000 hours or 7 years on social media (assuming you start around age 10, which seems normal in houses that aren't mine).

Here is where I become a broken record about spending intentionally, but in this case with your time. We all "waste" time watching TV, movies, sports, etc., but life is short and the more we can spend our time intentionally and with actual people, the happier we will be. This isn't a book about happiness or social media's effects on your happiness, there are countless others who are much better suited to write about that, but when we are spending 2.5 hours per day primarily looking at what we think is "real," it's not healthy for our wealth. It's hard enough dealing with the comparisons to our physical neighbors, colleagues, etc., but with social media it's exponentially worse. Teddy Roosevelt was right about comparison being the thief of joy, but it's also the thief of wealth and our most precious resource, time.

Aside from spending your time intentionally, I would also encourage you to adjust your perspective and zoom out. It's been researched that astronauts who return from space have a better appreciation for life and are less bothered by the daily minutia compared to the rest of us. The same principle holds true here. In this strange bubble where I live it would be easy for me to think that everyone drives a luxury car or lives in a 4,000 square foot house, because that's what I'm surrounded by. For example, the median household income in my town is a staggering $250,000, but if I zoom out to the median U.S. household income it's approximately $70,000. If I zoom out further, there are developing countries where the median household income is only hundreds of dollars per year. Perspective! It's easy to think that your bubble, whether like mine or drastically different, is normal, reframing and zooming out will help you to be grateful for what you have instead of constantly wanting what you don't.

GAMBLING VS. INVESTING

Another difficult part of our world is everything we constantly read, hear, and see about people who have made millions quickly off some sort of "investment." The media loves these stories and the clickbait headlines that they generate, but the media rarely talks about those who lost everything. We constantly hear about the Dogecoin millionaires, the Bitcoin Family, a family who invested their entire life savings in Bitcoin and now travels the world on their fortune, or those who invested early in Tesla because they believed in Elon Musk. Before I go any further, let me say, good for these people. I don't begrudge anyone wealth, regardless of how it's attained. Let me also say that this isn't investing. This is luck. It's no different than going to Las Vegas and placing your life savings on black at the roulette wheel. I mentioned earlier that I was "lucky" with my golf condo, which was true, because I had no plan and no idea how to invest. This was also a gamble that paid off, although not nearly to the same extent as being an early Bitcoin or Tesla investor. I'm not saying that gambling or experimenting shouldn't be part of your portfolio, by all means, but let's limit the downside. This is why I allocate 10% to alternative investments or individual stocks. The problem is that the media makes it sound like every overnight millionaire made a great investment and we rarely hear about those who gambled it all and lost. Also, on the rare occasion that we do hear those stories, the entire tone is different. The crypto millionaire "invested in Bitcoin during the early days," but the people who lost all of their money on some altcoin were "gambling their future" or "scammed." Hindsight is always 20/20 and what was a gamble then may be reported as a "great investment decision" years later.

Investing takes time and patience and let me walk through a few examples of what happens when the roulette ball lands on red. First, let's relive my childhood growing up in the 80s and 90s (apologies for any younger readers, but bear with me). When I was a kid and through my early 20s, I loved going to Blockbuster video and renting a movie. This is how my now wife and I spent a lot of our dating years. For those of you who have no idea what it means to go to a store and rent a movie just think about Netflix when I mention Blockbuster. At its peak in 2004, Blockbuster had $6B in revenue, the equivalent of $9B in 2022. There were also 9,000 Blockbuster video locations, which is close to the number of Dunkin' stores there are in the U.S. today. Blockbuster also employed almost 100,000 people! Lastly, in 2000 Netflix was offered to Blockbuster for $50M, but Blockbuster laughed them out of the room. The same way that people talk about investing in Netflix today is similar to how they felt about Blockbuster then. In 2010, only 10 years after laughing at Netflix and 6 years after record revenue, they filed for bankruptcy. For those people who had their life savings invested in Blockbuster, ticker symbol, BLIAQ, they lost everything as the stock price tumbled from close to $30/per share to worthless.

Let's continue to focus on stocks for a bit longer. In today's stock market most of the trading is conducted by algorithms that are analyzing hundreds of thousands of pieces of information or more to determine if they should buy or sell Microsoft, Google, Meta, Netflix, etc. You are likely not smarter than these algorithms, so don't try to be. I was fortunate to learn this lesson when I was much younger. My parents, again amazing, allowed me to open an investment account when I was a teenager. I loved researching companies and still love researching, even though I had no idea what I was actually reading (try handing an annual report to an adult let alone a teenager and see how it goes!). So here I was with an account, dial-up internet, and a computer, what could possibly go wrong? Turns out, everything! I "invested" in a number of "can't miss" stocks based on my careful analysis. One of those stocks was America Online Latin America, ticker symbol AOLA. For those of you who are around my age (40s), you will remember America Online or AOL, which was the Facebook of our generation. America Online Latin America was simply an offshoot to take advantage of the internet growth in the developing markets of South America. If you have no idea what I'm talking about, this time, it's not because you are younger than I am, but rather that the company no longer exists. Much like Blockbuster, it went bankrupt. This lesson hurt at the time, both my ego and my teenage wallet, but in hindsight I was fortunate that AOLA and the handful of other companies that I "invested" in went bankrupt because otherwise I may have thought I was actually good at this, and I likely would have kept trying to pick winners when the stakes were higher later in life.

For a present day example, let's talk about Google. I love Google. We have Google phones, too many smart speakers, cell service through GoogleFi, Nest thermostats, etc. I am intentionally spending on Google! That being said, I have no idea if Google will be around in 5, 10, or 20 years and if it is still around, I secondly have no idea how successful it will be. This is why I purchase thousands of companies through index funds which I discussed earlier. Some of these companies will thrive and grow, like I think Google will, and some will fail like AOLA, but I have no idea how to truly weed out the winners from the losers, nor the time to do so, which is why I simply purchase all of them. An individual stock's return may significantly exceed that of the total market average, but with that potential comes significantly greater risk.

PATIENCE TAKES CONFIDENCE

If you've ever played a sport, you know that results don't happen overnight. It takes time to build your hand eye coordination, muscle memory, endurance, etc. I played sports for the majority of my young life and like most, I remember winning fondly, losing bitterly, and practicing as simply necessary.

This walk to wealth is the same with one exception. You now have the answers to the test! In other words, you can win this game of wealth, but you still need to put in the work to get there. All of those practices from my youth may have been drastically different if I didn't view them as something "necessary," something to merely get through, but rather the means to a win. If I knew that my coaches were having me practice the exact right skills that would lead to certain victory, I wouldn't have been in such a rush to get through it.

When I was 11-years-old, I loved playing two-hand-touch football in the street with my friends (this is the early 90s and pre the popularity of flag football). I begged my parents to let me sign up to play tackle football and of course they did. I remember showing up to my first practice and thinking I would be the star of my team given my prowess for two-hand-touch, only to find out that I was about 5 inches shorter and 20 lbs. lighter than my teammates which frankly felt like Ant-Man battling Hulk. During these practices I felt more like a tackling dummy than a football player. It all felt pointless, but I asked to sign up and so I went, week after week. I rarely, if ever, had a chance to play in the actual games and didn't get an ounce better, but not from lack of trying, but rather lack of practicing the right things. I was simply part of the drills, but never learned anything from them. It was like an out of body experience, only one where your body gets a lot of bruises! I showed up for every practice and every game because I had made a commitment, but I likely would have taken more from those seemingly pointless drills if they weren't so, well, seemingly pointless.

As the basketball player, Allen Iverson, famously said, "We talking about practice. Not a game. Not the game that I go out there and die for and play every game like it's my last. Not the game. We talking about practice, man." Yes, that is exactly what we are talking about, because in this case, what you are learning about saving, investing, and money babies will lead to certain wealth if you are patient, especially at times when it's not easy because you want to reactivate your account to binge the latest Netflix series, sign up for the gym again, or because you think "this time is different" when the stock market drops by 50%. My hope is that you will have the confidence in your plan to be patient and stay the course!

Everything we've talked about on this walk is built on the notion of being an active participant in your journey towards wealth, but that doesn't mean being an active trader. As we discussed earlier, active mutual fund managers who trade individual stocks for a living can rarely achieve results that are superior to the average stock market return, and when they do, it's even rarer for them to repeat that feat. You may remember that the first point in my personal philosophy was "Never Sell" and even the most confident investor needs a reminder when their account value drops by 50%!

We've all had arguments in our lives, whether with a sibling, friend, spouse, parent, etc. Occasionally, those arguments escalate, and we say things that we regret and, in some cases, words that are impossible to ever pull back. This is the "I never want to speak to you again," "I hate you," or something far worse and it's the same with your wealth. If you panic and sell during a sudden market decline or change your approach based on the latest expert predicting the next crash instead of trusting your plan, you will likely be in a situation that causes irreversible, or at a minimum years' worth of damage to your wealth. Wealth takes decades to create, but can be destroyed in a single day!

SIMPLE STEP 4 – SUMMARY OF ACTIONS (PLAN)

Let's summarize our actions for the third SIMPLE step, Patience, on our walk to wealth. This walk requires confidence which stems from belief in your PLAN:

- **P**atience – This is a long walk to wealth and not an overnight gamble to get rich quick.

- **L**ifestyle Inflation – Keeping up with the Joneses is the one of the surest ways to derail your plan to wealth and happiness.

- **A**nswers – Success requires confidence in your plan which comes from knowing that you have the answers to the test.

- **N**o action – Once you've created your plan and automated the process, taking no additional actions will often yield the best results. Ignore the noise!

CHAPTER FIVE: SIMPLE STEP 5 – LEARN

"An investment in knowledge pays the best interest."

Benjamin Franklin

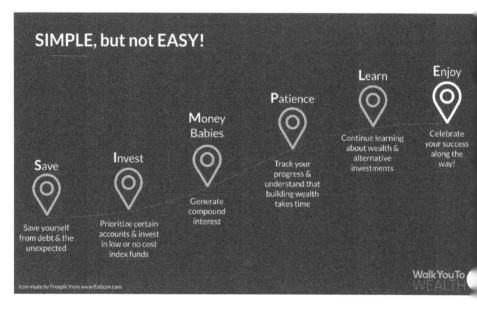

Along this walk, it's critical to never stop learning. The world of personal finance and investment opportunities has evolved more over the past decade than possibly ever in history. The cost of investing in the stock market has gone from approximately $15 per transaction to free, Bitcoin was created, spawning an entirely new investment opportunity, and the world of crowdfunding has opened up investments that were previously reserved for institutions or wealthy individuals. This doesn't mean that you should invest in every new idea, but rather, continue to learn because you never know what may be a good opportunity for the 10% of your portfolio that you may choose to allocate towards alternative investments. This learning may come in the form of online articles, podcasts, books, or your own mistakes. In this section, I will share some of my learnings along the way, including my biggest financial regrets, which are often the most painful and valuable lessons.

NET WORTH & PASSIVE INCOME

I remember texting my wife "we passed $1M!" to which she replied, "Great, what time are you coming home from work?" Talk about taking the air out of my balloon! I was talking about our net worth, which is just a basic calculation of how much you are worth as of a certain date. You simply add up the value of all your stuff, or assets, and subtract all the money you owe, or your liabilities. I don't bother adding up my sneakers with the holes in them or my precious American Giant sweatpants, but you certainly can include literally everything. I try to keep it simple with my cash, investments, and real estate. For most of us, one of our biggest assets will be our primary home. Your house is not an investment, but it is an asset. This is oddly one of the more hotly debated topics in the world of personal finance and it baffles me. There are some people who will exclude their house from their net worth based on the logic that they will need to live somewhere, which is true, but that doesn't change the fact that it's an asset. What I mean is that you own it, or at least part of it, and it could be sold for value, so therefore it's an asset and should be included in your net worth calculation; however, I do agree that it's not an investment. An investment's sole purpose is to produce revenue or increase in value, where your home's sole purpose is to provide shelter. In summary, your primary residence is an asset, but not an investment.

Obviously if you have some priceless Beanie Babies, a Bob Ross original painting, Garbage Pail Kids cards, or anything else of significant value, feel free to include it. Mine is pretty basic, until which time my original Atari 2600 becomes highly sought after (apologies, but as a child of the 80s, it's a real source of pride). Once your assets are added together, you then focus on your liabilities. These typically include credit card debt, student loans, car loans, and mortgages. Your net worth is the difference between the two

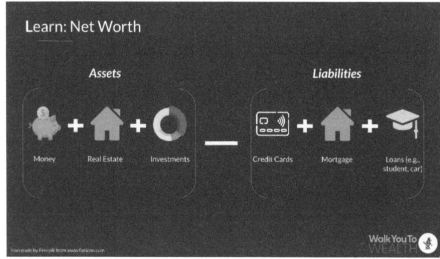

totals or total assets minus total liabilities. A typical and basic net worth calculation may look like this:

Your net worth may be positive or negative, and it is simply a snapshot as of a point in time to let you know if you are building wealth or losing it. I calculate my net worth annually on 12/31, simply to see any improvements from the prior year. It's a good indication of walking towards wealth.

Next, let's talk about some investing rules of thumb that are helpful. There is no magically perfect amount to target for retirement, but for a general rule of thumb, when your investable assets, such as stocks and bonds, reach 25X your expenses, that money should last approximately 30 years. In other words, if you spend $50,000 a year, you will need approximately $1.25M ($50,000*25) of investable assets in your portfolio to support that $50,000 of spending over the next 30 years, including an annual increase for inflation. This could allow you to ultimately leave your career or take a chance at pursuing a passion and is the rule of thumb that is used by the Financial Independence Retire Early, or FIRE community. This is known as the 4% rule and was first identified by the Trinity study which back tested a portfolio to determine a safe withdrawal rate for a typical retirement. This study determined that 4% was that rate or 25X your annual needs. This is a rule of thumb and should be taken as that, some people have even recommended being more aggressive and going as high as a 5% withdrawal rate and if you are more conservative, 3% may be a better number to use. Either way, 25X of what you want to live on is a good retirement goal to aim for. Personally, I use a 3% withdrawal rate, or 33X my annual needs, as my target which is conservative and may result in me working unnecessarily longer than I need to, but that's the cost of peace of mind! As you get closer to retirement, you will want to get more precise about your situation or "measure twice and cut once" as carpenters say to make sure that you have enough assets and cash flow before you leave your career. In the meantime, the 25X or my personal 33X will give you a target to shoot for.

When determining your retirement goals, you also want to be aware of any passive income, which is even a buzzier term than side hustle. Passive income means a lot of different things to different people, mostly because it's good clickbait. To me, it's income that requires NO additional effort. This is a high bar and there aren't that many true sources of passive income that can pass this test. The best one, which we already discussed, is money babies in the form of dividends and bond interest. These are truly passive as the companies or institutions will pay you for your investment or loan. There is no effort required to earn that money which is what makes it passive. It also fits in with my asset allocation model. The ultimate goal is to build as much passive income as possible to offset your expenses and then you will be financially independent. Some other forms of passive income may include interest on a high yield savings account, staking cryptocurrency (using certain cryptocurrencies to validate transactions which helps the underlying blockchain network operate), social security, pensions, or interest from crowdfunded investments. There are also semi-passive income streams. These are income streams that are either front loaded with work, such as writing an e-book or creating an online learning course or require periodic work or reinvestment such as being a landlord. The more passive income you have the better, secondly, the more semi-passive income, and lastly active income which is your typical salaried or hourly job.

Another rule of thumb is the rule of 72. Essentially it is a quick way to figure out how long it will take for your investment to double in value based on the projected return. If we use the average stock market return of 10%, the rule of 72 tells us that it will take us approximately 7.2 years to double our investment (72/10). By comparison, if we are fully invested in short-term bonds and expect a return of 2%, it would take 36 years (72/2) to arrive at the same destination. As we've already discussed, very few investments have a consistent year-over-year return; however, this is an easy way to project potential future balances based on the expected return of your investments. There no perfect way to project returns because as we discussed earlier, no one really knows how the stock market or any other market will perform tomorrow let alone over the next 5, 10, or 36 years, but the rule of 72 provides a quick and general sense of how long it will take to double your money given various potential returns.

ALTERNATIVE INVESTMENTS

There are hundreds of thousands of investments available to you in today's economy, some of which provide great returns and some of which we covered earlier during our discussion on investment options. Below are only a few of them, along with my perspective on each one which I'm continuing to learn about:

Crowdfunding – Crowdfunding sites and apps have grown significantly in popularity in recent years. These sites allow investors to pool their money together to make a purchase that would typically only be possible by an extremely wealthy individual or company. Some of these options are only available to what's known as an accredited investor. This is a fancy term for someone who had an annual income exceeding $200,000 over the last two years, or a net worth of $1M or more. The general idea behind this rule is that these people are more sophisticated, and therefore, can make investments that are less regulated and potentially riskier. Some of the more popular crowdfunding investments involve real estate. This may be a collection of single-family homes, or commercial property, such as office buildings, or farmland. This real estate is jointly owned by the "crowd" and then the income from these investments is distributed back to the owners in proportion to their ownership percentage. You can also invest in fine art through a site such as Masterworks, personal loans, restaurants, privately held companies, or almost anything else you can think of. These sites have opened up investment opportunities in a way that wasn't possible a few years ago. The upside is the access and opportunity to invest in a unique offering. The downside is that unlike the REITs we just discussed, or index funds, these markets are typically illiquid, meaning it may be difficult to sell in a hurry as there isn't a public exchange available. There are also typically higher fees associated with these investments as compared to traditional index funds; however, the upside could also be greater. Bottom line is that crowdfunding options are a unique and interesting alternative that is worth learning more about.

Cryptocurrency & Web3 – As mentioned earlier, cryptocurrency is a decentralized form of digital money so that you can essentially be your own bank. There are thousands of cryptocurrencies with varying levels of legitimacy as well as an entire ecosystem of related investment opportunities. The two most popular cryptocurrencies are Bitcoin and Ether. Let's just discuss these two as examples. Bitcoin is similar to a traditional currency in the sense that you can use it to make purchases where accepted; however, its value is determined by the demand for its fixed supply of 21M Bitcoins, unlike the supply of U.S. dollars which are controlled by the government, and therefore, limitless. The value of Bitcoin is extremely volatile. For example, over the last 10 years it's gone from $200 per Bitcoin to over $60,000 with lots of ups and downs in between. There are some who consider it to be more closely akin to gold, which is a commodity, rather than

141

a currency. Most importantly, it's decentralized, meaning that no single entity controls Bitcoin and it allows anyone to participate regardless of factors that can be limiting in the traditional banking world, such as gender, race, sex, etc. Ether by contrast is a cryptocurrency which is native to Ethereum, a decentralized platform which supports a variety of applications, including decentralized finance or DeFi apps. These are based on smart contracts or virtual agreements without the need for a third party. For example, if you've ever purchased a home, you understand all the parties involved from the deed transfer to your escrow account. Now think about if that process could be done safely and securely, but without those third parties and that's DeFi. The token or currency associated with Ethereum transactions is Ether or ETH. This is a fairly new world by investment standards. It's also highly volatile; however, it could be a significant disrupter. This technology has already and will continue to change the way we interact, communicate, play games, invest, and process financial transactions. Another popular example in this space are Non-Fungible Tokens, or NFTs. NFTs allow you to purchase something unique of which there is a limited supply or a single copy, such as digital art, which could be for personal enjoyment, special access, or as a collectible. The money bag logo for Walk You to Wealth is an NFT that I purchased to learn more about this technology. The most popular example has been the Bored Ape Yacht NFTs which sold for millions of dollars and allowed owners to participate in the Bored Ape Yacht Metaverse known as the Otherside. Each cryptocurrency (e.g., Bitcoin, Ether, Dogecoin) is generally supported by online communities of rabid supporters, not dissimilar to sports fans. Lastly, imagine organizations that are owned and managed by a community of people using the blockchain to vote on decisions without the need for traditional corporate leadership. These are known as Decentralized Autonomous Organizations, or DAOs. As I'm writing this, a DAO is attempting to purchase the Denver Broncos football team for $4B. Bitcoin, Ether, NFTs, Metaverse, and DAOs are only a small part of this world that is different, exciting, constantly evolving, and worth learning about as a potential investment for part of the 10% that you can afford to lose.

In summary, the world of investment options is evolving rapidly, and you should continue to learn and have fun by investing a small percentage of your money in something that interests you. If none of this or the other options interest you, then just allocate the 10% that was intended for alternatives to index funds, but it's nice to take a shot at something that you find intriguing. I track my minimal cryptocurrency investments more than my 70% in stock index funds, because I find the world and use cases to be fascinating. As I also mentioned earlier, I am researching some crowdfunding options in the farmland space. It doesn't mean that I can't get a better return for lower fees with an index fund, but this is the 10% that's about something you are interested in learning about because investing should also be fun. For me, it also helps to have a cap and know that there is a set percentage of money to invest in something different, like a 200-acre corn farm in Illinois or a cryptocurrency trying to help the millions of people who are unbanked in the world.

COLLEGE SAVINGS

If you have children and plan to pay for some or all of their higher education, there's a dedicated "Now" account for that known as a 529. These accounts allow you to invest after-tax dollars which can be used tax-free, along with their money babies, if they are used for qualified educational expenses. Benefits will vary by state so I would start by researching the plan that is available in your state. There are two primary items you want to know about: 1) are any of your contributions tax-deductible in your state? And 2) what are the fees associated with the account and underlying investments options? The good news is that both of these should be fairly easy to find through a quick Google search. For example, I'm invested in my home state plan of Massachusetts because they allow me to deduct up to $2,000 per year as a married filer, the 529 account itself has no fees, and it has index fund options with low expense ratios (back to those ridiculous percentage-based fees!). Due to the way that 529s are set up, I strongly recommend, and am personally invested in, the target date index fund option for my children. It works the same way as the target date funds that we spoke about earlier for retirement; however, instead of your retirement age, you would use the age your child will be going to college. In other words, if your son or daughter is starting college in 2040, you would want to choose the closest age-based index fund to that year. This fund will automatically become invested more conservatively as your child gets closer to that date. 529s are only one option, but the potential for state tax deductions, tax-free withdrawals, and low-cost target date index funds, make them one of the easiest and best solutions. If you have friends and family who want to help with the cost of college, they can also easily contribute, and every deposit into the account is automatically invested in the underlying fund you initially chose. This makes the process of automation even easier, because if you deposit funds, they are automatically invested without a second step, unlike the process we discussed earlier.

LIFE INSURANCE

Nobody, myself included, wants to think about their death. For me, this is definitely true and it's one of the reasons that buying life insurance is so difficult. The other reasons are the salesmen, complex options, high fees, and requirements, such as a physical examination. I won't use this section to write about the myriad of life insurance options, but rather, cover only a few basics. First, let's cover the need. Unless you are single with no children or independently wealthy (at which point you likely wouldn't be reading this!), you need life insurance. For most of us, the best type of life insurance, that's both straightforward and reasonable, is term life insurance. Term life insurance allows you to pay a set amount per month or year for a fixed amount of coverage. For example, if you're in your 20s and wanted to cover your family with a $500,000 benefit in the event of your death anytime over the next 20 years, it would cost you about $31 per month or $1 a day. This type of insurance can be obtained online through many reputable sites and often doesn't require a physical exam. I recently went through the site Lemonade for my term policy. This isn't an advertisement for them as there are many other similar companies, such as Haven Life and MassMutual. Regardless of which company you choose, it is just a few clicks of the mouse and you can be billed or charged automatically on your credit card so that you don't forget to pay the bill. You can also oftentimes obtain term life insurance for a reasonable cost through an employer or association of some kind. I also recommend and participate in my employer's plan. The only downside is that this type of insurance is usually tied to your employment and can only be maintained after a job separation at a higher premium or monthly payment. This is the same with an association's plan. As a Certified Public Accountant, I am a member of the American Institute of Certified Public Accountants and through my membership I qualify for low-cost term insurance; however, much like employer-based life insurance it's contingent on me being a member, which I may not always be. Now we understand the need and type, let's talk about the amount.

In terms of amount, there are numerous calculators online that will help you determine that, but essentially, it's a personal decision. For me, I want to make sure that my wife can afford to stay in our home and maintain our current lifestyle assuming that she is also working in her profession as a teacher. This goes back to the 4% rule we discussed earlier. This is the back of the envelope calculation for me: 25 x (annual expenses minus net income). To make this real, let's say we spend approximately $100,000 a year and my wife earns a net income of $50,000 a year as a teacher. My formula is 25 x ($100,000 - $50,000) which equals $1.25M of insurance. This is the approximate right amount for me to provide financial stability for my family as the primary earner. That being said, this will vary according to your needs and circumstances. For example, if you want to cover the cost of college for your children you may want to add that amount separately.

Last point, if you are fortunate enough to have a spouse or partner who stays at home, potentially caring for small children, they should also be insured with term life insurance. Although they aren't technically earning money, they are performing an important role that would need to be filled by daycare, a nanny, a cleaner, etc. In summary, if you have a family and especially if you have children, you should have life insurance, and the most straightforward and reasonable option is term insurance.

ACCOUNT SECURITY

The majority of my professional career has been about managing risk for a company, its customers, and shareholders. This however is about your personal risk. There are countless tips and actions that I could write about here, such as regularly checking your credit report, analyzing credit card transactions, having a dedicated laptop or device for financial transactions, and regularly reviewing bank statements for suspicious charges. These are great recommendations, except for the fact that most of us will never consistently do any of them! So instead, let's talk about practical steps that you may actually implement. You should use two-factor authentication, a password manager, never click on emailed or texted links, and understand the fraud reimbursement policy of the financial companies who maintain your accounts.

Let's start with two-factor authentication. If your financial company doesn't offer it as part of its standard log in process, then call and ask, as this varies from company to company. If they don't offer it at all, I would find a different company. Two-factor authentication simply requires two pieces of information to be used at log in, usually your password along with a passcode from an app or text, therefore, making it more difficult for your account to be compromised. This is a minor inconvenience when you log in but provides an additional layer of security. Two-factor authentication through a dedicated app is also better than text, but either is better than nothing.

The second practical tip is to use a password manager such as Google, 1Password, or Bitwarden (Google password managers for more options). Yes, all your passwords are now with a third party which carries its own risks and concerns, but they are also a heck of a lot more complicated than "Password1234!" or using the same basic one across multiple accounts. If you are like most people, you have a go-to password and then occasionally add an exclamation point or additional number if required by a new site. The shorter the password, the faster it will be compromised. These password management services will suggest a long and complicated password that is unique for each account. They will also autofill the password when you try to log in to the service, such as Amazon or Netflix. Again, there is a trade off as now Google, Bitwarden or whomever you choose to use has access to all your passwords, but in my opinion, that tradeoff is worth the risk compared to using basic, short, generic, and similar passwords across accounts.

Thirdly, let's discuss phishing. Phishing scams are when a seemingly well-known company, perhaps even one where you hold investments, sends you an email or text asking you to update some information by clicking a link. You may think, I would never fall for that, but again, these are highly sophisticated. I received one from what appeared to be the cryptocurrency exchange that I worked for, and it looked so realistic that I contacted our customer service team to see if I really needed to update information associated with my account. Fortunately, I knew enough not to click the link, but again, I work in risk management, and it was literally trying to spoof the company that I worked for, and it still looked good enough for me to question it! Another great example is from my time at my previous employer in traditional financial services when fraudsters sent customers an email that appeared to be from the company and when you clicked the link it opened a site that looked nearly identical to the company's log-in page. Gold star to these criminals because even after you used your actual credentials to log in to their fake site, they routed you to the real one so you would ideally never know that your login credentials were just compromised. Think about that for a second, you log in to a completely illegitimate site and behind the scenes it routes and logs you in to the real one. To avoid this, don't click on links. Navigate to the site in your web browser, preferably where it's saved as a favorite, and log in or contact customer service, but never click a link.

Lastly, review and understand your financial company's policy on fraudulent activity. For example, some companies will reimburse you only if there are criminal charges filed, so if your ex-husband or wife runs off with your money because he or she knows your password, you better be ready to file charges. Some companies will also not allow a reimbursement if you shared your password with a data aggregator tool, such as a budgeting site like Mint which requires you to connect your financial accounts. You don't need to know all the details about how your account is secured by the company, but you should understand their policy for customer reimbursements from fraud.

There is no such thing as 100% security in today's digital world, but the above are simple and practical steps to add a layer of protection to your financial life.

FINANCIAL MYTHS

As with any topic, there is no shortage of misinformation available on social media and online. Throughout this book, we've discussed most of these, so I won't go into great detail, but I want to highlight, and in some cases, reiterate, some of the biggest ones:

1) Credit cards are evil: Consumer debt can be devastating, but building credit and using a credit card responsibly should be part of your financial plan. Last year, my credit card points contributed

$1,500 to my emergency fund from purchases I was going to make anyway.

2) Buy low and sell high: No one can predict the top or the bottom of the stock, real estate, crypto, or any other market. Buy when you have the money and hold!

3) Investing is only for the rich: My boys invest $2 of their allowance each week in mutual funds that have no fees and no minimums. Investing is how you get rich, but it's not reserved for only those who started that way!

4) Money can't buy happiness: Life is easier and more enjoyable with money. If you don't believe me or the independent study cited earlier, try it both ways and see which you prefer!

5) A house is a great investment: As we discussed, a house isn't an investment, but it's definitely an asset. Also, if you are using the 10-year rule, it can be a great asset.

6) Never pay off your mortgage because you can earn more in the stock market: This is up there with one of the biggest points of contention between "financial experts." Their logic is that it doesn't make financial sense to pay off your mortgage when the interest rate is significantly lower than the average stock market return of 10%. The math is

accurate, but the problem is twofold. First, we are comparing apples and oranges. An average and potential return in the stock market over the long-term is wildly different than a guaranteed return today. In this case, a more accurate comparison of a guaranteed return would be to compare your mortgage interest rate to other forms of guaranteed investments, like treasury bills or Certificates of Deposit (CDs), which in the recent past have returned less than 3%. I should also point out that all these rates change over time, back when my dad bought his first house mortgage rates were double digits, but so were the yields or returns on treasury bonds. Simply make sure you are comparing apples to apples from an investment perspective before you make a decision. The second and more important problem is that paying off a home is mostly psychological. It's not about math! If we only made decisions based on math, we would be robots! I paid off my rental property a few years ago which had an interest rate of 3.5% and at that time treasury bills were paying 1-2%. Yes, that money would have earned significantly more in the stock market, but more importantly, it felt like a weight was lifted off my shoulders after it was paid for.

7) It's too late to start: This is right up there with "I can't afford to start" which we discussed at the beginning of our walk. As I've said repeatedly and you will hear me echo when I discuss my financial regrets, the best time to invest was yesterday, but the next best time

is today! We can't jump in our DeLorean or hot tub time machine so the only way to fix this is to stop making excuses and start!

8) Taxes don't matter because I'm not part of the 1%: The lowest federal income tax bracket in the U.S. in 2022 is 10% and the highest is 37%. So yes, using tax-advantaged accounts helps those who are in the top bucket more than the lowest, but 10% is still worth prioritizing your accounts to take advantage of not paying more than you need to.

READ OR LISTEN

I've spent a fair amount of time listening to audiobooks about personal finance and I don't think I will ever stop learning something new. Much like what we've learned throughout our walk, there is no such thing as a perfect book, but below are some of my favorites to date:

Unshakeable by Tony Robbins and Peter Mallouk: I never thought I would recommend a book by Tony Robbins as he always seemed like the Richard Simmons of the life coaching world, but this book is terrific. It's filled with great tips, information, and insights from some of the best investors of our generation.

Elements of Investing by Burton G. Malkiel and Charles D. Ellis: This is a straight to the point guide that quickly and easily covers all the basics.

Random Walk Down Wall Street by Burton G. Malkiel: This book is long, but provides timeless advice and information about investing.

The Wealthy Gardener by John Soforic: This is the only personal finance book I've ever successfully got my wife to read! Enough said!

The Automatic Millionaire by David Bach: This book explains the importance of automating your investments and allowing time to generate money babies in a non-technical way.

The Millionaire Next Door by Thomas J. Stanley: This is an old classic and will open your eyes to the fact that the millionaires are often hidden unlike the debtors who are often masquerading as millionaires.

I Will Teach You to Be Rich by Ramit Sethi: This book is well written, practical, and easy to listen to. A great read for the younger generation!

Quit Like a Millionaire by Kristy Shen and Bryce Leung: A great personal story that brings the technical lessons of investing to real life.

Your Money Your Life by Vicki Robin and Joe Dominquez: This is potentially the original FIRE book, before the movement existed and a must read.

Meet the Frugalwoods by Elizabeth Willard Thames: A great storyteller whose extreme frugality will make you cringe at times, but will also make you think twice about your own spending.

The Psychology of Money by Morgan Housel: Arguably the best, and definitely one of the most accessible, books about money.

FINANCIAL REGRETS

Hopefully all the information above has been helpful, increased your financial awareness, and simplified the overly complicated process of creating wealth. Now, I want to share some of my financial regrets so that you can learn from my mistakes.

1) Not being financially literate. As I mentioned at the outset of our walk, I don't know everything, but I wish I knew at 20 what I have learned by 40. The difference financially in those 20 years could have been tremendous to my financial wellbeing and wealth. My boys started earning an allowance around the age of five and I quickly introduced them to saving and investing. They also learned a lot about spending intentionally. How do I know? I once sat on the sideline and watched them debate about purchasing a souvenir at an amusement park for about 15 minutes. It was comical, but I realized that they were quickly learning about spending their money intentionally. They learned about delayed gratification too, as they would save up for certain toys and self-regulate their spending (they hated to have less than $100 in their wallet!). They also allocate $2 of their $7 allowance to their own brokerage accounts, and we go through the clicks of

investing together. They were, and still are, excited about doing it together and during our first few weeks of it they would constantly ask if they owned every company we passed in the car, such as Starbucks, Walmart, Mobile, etc. This is when I first mentioned to them the concept of money babies, all of which solidified the basics of investing at a young age. I remember being with them one Saturday afternoon waiting in line to return a lava lamp at Walmart when my oldest said, "Dad, don't we own Walmart?" to which I replied, "Yes," and then he said, "Well, why can't we skip this line?" I don't know how all of this will translate to their adult lives, but I like to think that they are headed in the right direction on their own walk to wealth because they know more about investing than some adults and certainly much more than I knew at their ages. Although it's never too late to start, I regret that I didn't know enough at 22 when I started working my first full time job about which funds to pick in my 401k, how to take advantage of free money, or about various investment options. I didn't fully understand the value of money babies at a young age and also felt lost in the sea of choices without anyone to help steer the ship. All the remaining regrets are simply pieces of this first one. If I knew more, had a plan, an investment philosophy, most, if not all, of the rest of these could have been avoided.

2) Not being financially uncomfortable. When I sold my condo in Myrtle Beach, it seemed like selling it

was the only way that my wife and I could afford to buy our condo in Boston. In hindsight, it was the only way that we could "comfortably" afford to buy our new home. Although the rental income from the golf condo was far from life changing money, we could have easily paid it off by now and simply been receiving a check every month, with minimal effort given that the management company handled most of the work. The point is, if there is a time to take chances and be financially uncomfortable, it's when you are younger and have fewer responsibilities. Another much more financially devastating decision was not investing in Bitcoin when I first learned about it through work in 2015 when the price was around $300 per Bitcoin. We had just moved into a new house, my wife was no longer working, we had two children and again it seemed like every dollar mattered so much. My natural loss aversion also kicked in. This is where the 10% alternative allocation could have gone a long way with prices ranging from $16,000-$60,000 per Bitcoin over the last few years. Now, of course, hindsight is 20/20, but this isn't about the explosion of Bitcoin or golf condos, but rather, about being comfortable being financially uncomfortable.

3) Not buying a second rental property in Boston. As I mentioned earlier, a large percentage of my net worth comes from my primary residence and rental property in Boston. During the almost 10 years that my wife and I lived in Boston, I wish we had the

foresight to move into a new condo and start renting ours. This would have put us in a position of having two rental properties in the city now. Much like my previous regret, we were likely too financially naïve and comfortable. We also didn't have a financial plan which would have forced us to discuss if we wanted to be landlords and what that would mean.

4) Not contributing sooner to a Roth IRA and Health Savings Account (I). As I mentioned earlier, the Never and Now accounts should be your first priority after free money, but again, I didn't have a prioritization board game when I was younger. These different accounts seemed confusing, almost like learning a foreign language, even during my early days working at a financial services company. As we discussed earlier, the sooner you start investing in these accounts, the sooner you can leverage the power of compounding your tax-free money babies. Specific to the HSA, a number of years ago, my employer at the time, started offering a high deductible health plan with access Ian HSA account, but I didn't take advantage of this benefit right away. To make matters worse, when I finally signed up for the high deductible health In and HSA, I used most of my contributions for medical expenses instead of investing the money. I tell you this so that you can learn from my mistakes and if you have access to a high deductible health plan with an HSA and can afford to do so, take advantage of it.

5) Not contributing sooner to 529s. You are hopefully sensing a theme about time at this point, but here is another spot where I failed to see the huge benefits of contributing a small amount when my kids were born and allowing the power of money babies to do the rest. The only way to offset the loss of time from generational money babies is to contribute more later. Losing time is an expensive mistake to make.

6) Not paying myself first. Most of us work too hard and too long not to learn this lesson early on. We all have bills to pay but remember to pay yourself first. The best and easiest way to do this is to automate your direct deposit based on the account prioritization from the earlier chapter and remember that owning Amazon, Walmart, Target, Netflix, Disney, etc., is much better than owing them.

7) Not spending intentionally. This is one that is still a struggle, but I've certainly tried to become better in recent years. I've tried to prioritize spending on family vacations, experiences, and also just spending time with my family without the need for a dinner or lunch out. Despite my progress, I can't help but look around any room in my house and see hundreds of dollars of unintentional stuff. The pandemic has taught many lessons, but for me it's that the more time I am lucky enough to spend with my family, the more time I want to spend with them. This is my primary "Why?" for investing.

8) Staying at my job too long. I mentioned earlier that I spent 15 years at my previous company, which was a great company to work for with lots of terrific benefits, including a best-in-class 401k match, but I should have been more active in managing my career. I was always willing to leave, but never pursued it actively enough. Leaving my job ultimately allowed me to significantly increase my compensation, which as we know is limitless.

SIMPLE STEP 5 - SUMMARY OF ACTIONS (GAIN)

Let's summarize our actions for the fourth SIMPLE step, Learn, on our walk to wealth. This walk requires you to GAIN continuous knowledge and learn from your mistakes:

- **G**row - Investments are continually evolving, and if you are interested, you should embrace learning and experimenting to grow your knowledge.

- **A**lternative - There are 1000s of alternative investments that 10% of your money could be allocated to as a way to learn and make mistakes without risking your future–

- **N**et Worth - Calculating your net worth on an annual basis is an easy way to track your walk to wealth.

CHAPTER SIX: SIMPLE STEP 6 – ENJOY

"Wealth is not his that has it, but his that enjoys it."

Benjamin Franklin

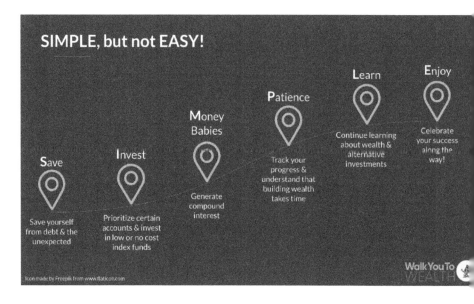

A few years ago, I coached my kids' soccer team. I know relatively nothing about soccer, but fortunately, I am pretty good at entertaining kids and also know that the more they run, the better! At practice I would always talk about superheroes, because there aren't many kids who can't relate to Spiderman, Hulk, Flash, or Wonder Woman. We would play countless games where they would scream like the Hulk, race like Flash, or chase me like the Avengers. My boys never liked soccer, but they showed up every week and seemed to have fun at practice. They kept coming back because even though they didn't love the sport, they were having fun and most importantly they always celebrated the end of the game with popsicles!

This walk to wealth is SIMPLE, but it's not easy. It requires time, thought, patience, and most importantly, sacrifice. That's why it's essential to also have fun and celebrate significant milestones along the way. These may include opening your emergency fund, your first investment, the first time you contribute the maximum amount to an investment account, buying a home, or paying off a mortgage. Celebrations may include dinner, having a glass of wine, planning a vacation, etc. Sometimes these celebrations can be simply acknowledging what you've accomplished with a parent, friend, or spouse. When we paid off our condo, my wife and I talked about it, and both felt oddly relieved. I say "oddly" because our mortgage payment was offset by the rent, but this is the personal and psychological side of the equation. These celebrations or simple acknowledgements allow you to take a breath before moving on to the next goal. I'm convinced that if you don't stop to enjoy a popsicle, you likely won't show up to play the next week!

Another key factor for continuing on your walk and enjoying your wealth is to figure out your why. Why do you want to walk to wealth? This is a question that I can't answer for you, but I can tell you what motivates me to keep putting one foot in front of the other as well as what I've found to be some major motivating factors for others.

Financial Independence – This is a major motivator for me. In its simplest form, it means to have accumulated enough wealth that you can comfortably enjoy a life without needing to work. For me, this is about spending more time with my family, having choice, and trying new things. It's also about not being tied to a required business trip or my phone for the latest work message. I want to spend more time with my family, which might be hard to imagine after this pandemic, but I do! I also want to follow my passion for walking others to wealth, of which this book is a step in that direction. Now that I have a family, it's harder to take a leap, like that golf condo in my 20s, without knowing that my family is financially secure and independent. This is also shaped by the fact that my mom passed away at the young age of 61 from lung cancer, despite never having smoked. Life is too short to not spend as much of it as possible on your own terms.

Retirement – This is a huge concern for me and most people. If I mention retirement to my brother or neighbor, I almost always get the same headshake, chuckle, and remark about working forever. This doesn't have to be the case and is a big reason why you can't afford not to invest. I've seen family members forced to move in late stages of life and make dramatic lifestyle changes due to lack of planning. I've also seen the stress of not knowing if they will have enough money for health procedures or long-term care.

Travel – I hate traveling, but I think I'm in the minority. You may want to save up for a once in a lifetime trip like an African safari, a trip to Bali, or taking the family to Disney World (having been twice, I can tell you that it might be cheaper to take them on the African safari!). By investing your money, you will be able to take that trip sooner than if you simply stuck it under your mattress.

164

Education – I've already discussed my thoughts and personal decision to pay for my children's education, but this is a costly and significant endeavor.

Charity – Nelson Henderson said, "The true meaning of life is to plant trees, under whose shade you do not expect to sit." This is the power that we have by applying to charitable donations what we've learned and discussed along this journey about investing and money babies. My wife and I have a charitable donor-advised fund which is called the Feig Family Foundation. Before you dismiss this as something only rich people do (and I don't blame you for that initial reaction), you should know that this account was free to set up, required no minimum deposit, and we use it to periodically donate small amounts which are then automatically invested in low-cost index funds. We also take advantage of my company's generosity which matches $500 of donations. Always start with free money! We distribute some of our contributions to various charitable causes, but more importantly, we let the bulk of our deposits generate money babies which will accumulate over time so that we can make a larger difference for the causes that we care about. A lot of the companies that I mentioned earlier have donor-advised funds that you can open, including Fidelity Investments, Charles Schwab, and Vanguard. Imagine being able to plant those seeds now so that one day someone less fortunate can benefit! This is the power of wealth! You can also donate stocks or bonds that you've held for more than one year which allows you to deduct the value of the securities at the time of the donation for tax purposes. In other words, let's say you invested $100 in a stock index fund that's now worth $1,000. If you donate that stock index fund, you can deduct $1,000 on your taxes even though it only cost you $100 originally.

These are only a small handful of reasons to walk to wealth, and you will need to find what motivates you, but I can guarantee you already know what it is, otherwise you wouldn't be reading this book!

If you are fortunate enough to have someone else walking with you, you will also need to be on the same page otherwise you will likely never reach your destination. My wife and I discuss our financial goals on a regular basis. She has no interest in being involved in the details of account types, balances, index funds, etc. as she would rather talk about the kids than our net worth, and that's completely fine. Where I make sure we are aligned is on the big decisions, such as paying off our condo, prioritizing the boys' education accounts, and the fact that I'm planning to reach financial independence by age 47. Every relationship is different, and your spouse or partner may want to be more or even less involved than mine, but at a minimum you should ensure that you are charting your walk to wealth together. This alignment will help you stay on the path when times are hard and also avoid conflict about financial priorities. For example, if my wife felt strongly that the boy's should pay their own way through college, I would want to make sure that we agreed on an approach before I started investing in a 529 education savings account. My point is that you need to be aligned on these bigger financial goals, and in some cases the specific steps you are taking to get there, otherwise I might be saving in a 529 education account for an expense that we aren't planning to pay for, which wouldn't be the best use of my money, especially after the 10% penalty for withdrawals that aren't for qualified educational expenses!

When you reach financial independence, you will want to be aware of the tax consequences of your withdrawals. I know, talking more about taxes seems like the least enjoyable topic to put in a chapter about joy. The good news is that in our imperfect solution, the simplest way to think about this is in reverse order from how we originally prioritized the accounts with one minor change. If you remember back to our earlier chapter on investing, we prioritized funding in the following order:

1. Never - Pay Taxes Never

2. Now - Pay Taxes Now

3. Later - Pay Taxes Later

4. Always - Pay Taxes Always

In terms of spending, we will simply reverse the order with a slight modification:

1. Always - Pay Taxes Always

2. Later - Pay Taxes Later

3. Now - Pay Taxes Now

★ Never - Pay Taxes Never

Let me explain the high-level logic and also understand that your situation is different, so you should view these as general guidelines. We are starting our withdrawals from the Always account. The reason to start here is simply because some of this money is going to be taxed regardless in the form of the money babies we discussed earlier. In other words, if your spending is more than the amount of money babies that will be distributed via dividends and interest from your Always account, then simply set your Always account dividends and interest to cash instead of the reinvestment option. Again, you are going to be taxed on this distribution anyway, so why not use it, if you need it! Assuming you need more than the dividends and interest to live off of, and most of us will, now it becomes a question of tax brackets. In general, I would recommend continuing to withdraw from the Always account, assuming your long-term capital gains tax rate is lower than your ordinary income tax rate.

From the Always account, we move to the Later account. You should know that even if you don't want to withdraw from this account, the federal government will make you through what's known as Required Minimum Distributions (RMDs) at a certain age. Later accounts were titled as such given that we would owe taxes at a later date, and RMDs are essentially the government's way of making sure they get paid. Withdrawals from these accounts will always be taxed at your ordinary income level, so the hope is that you are in a lower income tax bracket now compared to when you were working; however, that may not be the case. Either way, this is our next stop.

168

The next account that you want to withdraw from is your Now account. We've already paid our taxes and are not required to withdraw any amount of money from this account. This money will continue to compound and earn money babies tax-free. Personally speaking, I view my Now account as my retirement insurance policy. What I mean is that by using this account last, it will ensure a healthy sum of tax-free money that I can use in the event of unexpected costs during my later years.

Lastly, our Never account. To reap the true benefits of never paying taxes, you should use this account to pay for qualified medical expenses in retirement. The reason this account doesn't have an order is that it will be used throughout retirement. As an added benefit you can also withdraw from it for non-qualified medical expenses, but you lose the never paying taxes aspect, which is critical to why we prioritized this account in the first place. There is not likely to be a shortage of medical expenses during these years as we discussed during the prioritization exercise and this account is how to pay for them tax-free.

Equally, if not more critical than what accounts to withdraw from, is what assets to sell down as part of the withdrawal. In other words, if you are withdrawing 4% of your portfolio, what funds should you sell? My simple answer is the previous years' winner. For example, if U.S. stocks are up significantly while the international stock market and bonds are down or flat, I would sell domestic stocks. If both U.S. and international stocks have gone down, I would take my withdrawal from bonds. If all assets are down, I would either leverage some of my reserve cash or sell in proportion to the decline in each asset to maintain my asset allocation. The main point is that our human nature tells us to sell the losers and keep the winners, but in this case, we want to do the opposite to fund our retirement or spending.

Finding your why, celebrating your wins, and having family agreement, coupled with written goals and automation, will help you on this walk.

SIMPLE STEP 6 - SUMMARY OF ACTIONS (WAY)

Let's summarize our actions for our sixth SIMPLE step, Enjoy, on our walk to wealth. This walk is long and requires you to find your own WAY of staying motivated:

- **W**hy - Finding your why requires figuring out what wealth means to you.

- **A**lways celebrating - Celebrate small victories, such as your first $10 deposit into your emergency fund and big victories like conquering credit card debt. Popsicles are great motivators!

- **Y**ou - Only you can figure out how best to stay motivated, but it's helpful to have a supportive and aligned family.

CHAPTER SEVEN: SIMPLE STRATEGIES BY AGE

"You can't go back and change the beginning, but you can start where you are and change the ending."

C.S. Lewis

We've discussed a lot during this walk and the following set of guidelines provide walk you to wealth steps that are tailored for each age group. Before we get into the details, it's important to reiterate that everyone's walk will be unique and your circumstances are personal, so you should adjust the below steps accordingly. For example, if you plan to retire at 50 instead of 65, then these guidelines will need to be adjusted to fit your specific situation, but I hope it provides a great framework for you as well as others in your life who you can help walk to wealth, whether it be friends, parents, or your own children.

	Age: 5-14 (allowance)
Save	Amount: 80-90% of allowance for toys, souvenirs, etc. Account: Wallet/Cash
Invest	Amount: 10-20% Account: Uniform Transfers of Minor Act (UTMA) Allocation: 100% stock
Money Babies	Low impact
Patience	Delayed gratification
Learn	Investing basics, intentional spending
Enjoy	First trade; owning known companies; having your own money

Walk You To WEALTH

My boys started earning an allowance at age five and I quickly introduced them to saving and investing. They also learned a lot about spending intentionally. How do I know? I remember my youngest constantly saying "I hate this part," when being asked to count his cash with his older brother to pay for whatever toy they decided to buy. The fact that he "hated" it, meant to me that he was learning about the value of money and intentional spending. They also started to learn delayed gratification as they would save up for certain toys. As I mentioned earlier, they also invest $2 of their allowance which has taught them so much about the world of investing.

At this age it's all about the basics, learning, and getting them excited. This could be as simple as them clicking to invest $2 in their own investment account or telling them insane stories about money babies!

My best parenting advice for raising financially literate children would be to openly discuss money in a kid-friendly way, explain investing in the stock market, tell them about money babies, and have them invest part of their allowance. Often money is a taboo topic in houses and that's where some of the problems start. This doesn't mean you should unload your financial stress onto your children, but my wife and I will openly talk about the stock market, filing our taxes, paying bills, or if something unexpected happens, such as those condo assessments I mentioned earlier. We are simply trying to normalize this entire world at a young age. My eight-year-old has even figured out how to check the stock market from his school iPad and regularly provides me with updates on the market. I discussed earlier that my oldest son and I wrote a book about money babies when he was five, after I used the term to describe compound interest. Below is our story with his cover art:

"One day a long, long, long, long, long, time ago, Mr. Dollar was feeling lonely. Mr. Dollar checked himself into the "savings account" for treatment. He was hoping that the institution could cure his loneliness. Once inside, his belly began to grow and grow, and Mr. Dollar felt a new feeling…happiness. After several months, Mr. Dollar's belly was huge! Then it happened! One magical day Mr. Dollar gave birth to three shining baby girls that he named Penny, Dime, and Nickel. Mr. Dollar asked Mr. Bank if he could move into a larger account so that he would have enough room for his growing family. Mr. Bank happily obliged. After several months in their new account, Mr. Dollar received the happiest news of his life. His three girls, Penny, Dime, and Nickel were all pregnant. The End."

Now you've received two books for the price of one! The above will never be confused with Moe Willems or any other famous children's author, but it was fun, we wrote it together, and it resonated with my kids, which is the most important part.

In terms of allowance, we've gone back and forth as parents from paying for specific chores to simply paying them allowance. Ultimately, we landed on simply paying them an allowance. We found that when we were paying for specific chores it was having an unintended outcome of my kids thinking that we would pay them for just about everything instead of them simply helping as a member of the family. For us, regardless of why they were paid, the key has been having them invest a portion of their allowance to build that "muscle memory." The $2 that my kids invest each week is in their Uniform Transfers of Minors Act (UTMA) account. This account is controlled by an adult and becomes the child's account at a specific age, typically 18 in most states. In the long run, I'm hopeful that what we've done as parents will result in financially literate adults one day, but the jury is still out for now!

Age: 15-20 (earned wages)	
Save	Amount: 80-90% for spending Account: Cash & online bank Debt: Avoid credit card debt
Invest	Amount: 10-20% Account: Custodial Roth IRA or Roth IRA Allocation: 100% stock
Money Babies	Moderate impact
Patience	Delayed gratification
Learn	Account types, paying yourself first, written goals
Enjoy	First job; earned wages

Walk You To
WEALTH

Everything in the above section can be carried down to this age group as well. The most important additional step at this age is to avoid credit card debt and unnecessary "joneses expenses" such as a fancy car.

Something else to consider as a parent is a Custodial Roth IRA. This is simply a Now account or Roth IRA for children who have earned income (e.g., babysitting, dog walking, snow shoveling). The idea of being able to start contributing to a Now account and earning money babies at such a young age, especially if there is some added incentive like a parental match, is huge! When my boys were 10 and 8, they were asked to help a neighbor with some of his yard work, mostly collecting sticks, weeding, and playing with his dog, but he paid them each $20 an hour. This is when we first opened their Custodial Roth IRAs. The time to create generational money babies is a huge advantage even if the starting amount is minimal. If your 15-year-old son or daughter invested $2,000 in a Custodial Roth IRA, they would have almost $235,000 of tax-free money at age 65, assuming a 10% return! That's mind blowing! I wish I could go back in time and invest some money from my summer job as a cashier at Booth Memorial Hospital in New York.

THE 20s

	Age: 20s
Save	Amount: 3 months of essential expenses Account: Online bank Debt: Eliminate and/or avoid credit card debt
Invest	Amount: 10%-30% of gross salary Accounts: By prioritization & automated Allocation: 90% boring, 10% fun
Money Babies	Very high impact
Patience	Delayed gratification; avoid lifestyle inflation
Learn	Net worth; learn about alternatives; term life insurance; automation
Enjoy	Eliminated credit card debt; emergency fund

Walk You To WEALTH

This is likely when you have your first "real" job. It is also the first decade of very high impact money babies. The reason being is that you are hopefully earning a full-time salary as opposed to a summer job and you still have

177

adequate time for decades of money babies. A $100 investment can turn into approximately $5,000 over 40 years. Think about that for a second. Let's assume we invest $1,200 per year ($100/month) during our 20s, so for ten years, and then never invest again. At 65, you would have approximately $537,000 from a total investment of $12,000!

Now, once you've developed the habit of saving $1,200 per year in your 20s, let's assume you kept going until 65 instead of stopping after 10 years, in that case you would have almost $863,000!

This perfectly illustrates the magic of very high impact money babies which come from the combination of higher income and time.

THE 30s

	Age: 30s
Save	Amount: 3-6 months of essential expenses Account: Online bank Debt: Eliminate and/or avoid credit card debt
Invest	Amount: 10%-30% of gross salary Accounts: By prioritization & automated Allocation: 90% boring, 10% fun
Money Babies	Very high impact
Patience	Delayed gratification; avoid lifestyle inflation
Learn	Net worth; alternatives; term life insurance; 529s, if applicable
Enjoy	Last decade of very high impact money babies; increased emergency fund; protecting your family with term life

WalkYouTo
WEALTH

This is your last decade of very high impact money babies given the combination of high salary and time to accumulate. The other focal points of this period may be building your emergency fund, opening 529s if you have children and plan to pay for some or all of their future education, and also evaluating term life insurance needs. You may also be purchasing your first home or upgrading to a new home. If so, keep the ten-year rule in mind as you make that purchase.

These are very high impact years, and you need to make sure that you avoid lifestyle inflation, especially as you likely start to earn more in your 30s than you had previously. It also may be a time of significant change, potentially with marriage or children. Prioritizing investing will provide tremendous returns in your 30s. Let's keep circling back to our $1,200 per year which would now turn into approximately $325,000 by age 65 if you started at 30! This is a tremendous amount of money, but also a lot less than the $863,000 from starting 10 years earlier.

Age: 40s	
Save	Amount: 3-6 months of essential expenses Account: Online bank Debt: Eliminate and/or avoid credit card debt; pay down mortgage
Invest	Amount: 10%-30% of gross salary Accounts: By prioritization & automated Allocation: 90% boring, 10% fun
Money Babies	High impact
Patience	Delayed gratification; avoid lifestyle inflation
Learn	Net worth; alternatives; term life insurance; 529s, if applicable
Enjoy	Being on the right track; increasing net worth; last decade of high impact money babies

Walk You To WEALTH

We've now officially left the decades of very high impact money babies, but the good news is that we are still in a high impact zone. Let's quickly go back to our previous example of saving $1,200 per year, which if we started at age 40 would result in approximately $118,000 at age 65. Still a lot of money, but let's think about this for a minute. This is less than half of your total from your 30s and also less than the total from investing only $2,000 from your summer job at 15! This isn't meant to discourage you, as you still have time, but if you are starting in your 40s, you will need to start playing catch up.

This may also be the time in your life where you start to think about paying down your mortgage. As I mentioned earlier, this is a decision that is often less about math and more about psychology. If you choose to pay off your primary residence, you should make sure that you want to remain there for a long period of time and also save up to pay it off in one lump sum or multiple large annual payments. The reason for accumulating one lump sum or at least larger annual chunks instead of adding more to your monthly payment is that once you give that money to the mortgage company you can't get it back if you need it. In other words, if you owe $200,000, it's much safer to set money aside each month in a traditional savings account just in case something catastrophic happens, like a sickness or job loss, while you are building the balance to pay off the mortgage.

Age: 50s	
Save	Amount: 3-6 months of essential expense, building more Account: Online bank Debt: Eliminate and/or avoid credit card debt; pay down mortgage
Invest	Amount: 10%-30% of gross salary Accounts: By prioritization & automated Allocation: 90% boring, 10% fun
Money Babies	Moderate impact
Patience	Delayed gratification; avoid lifestyle inflation
Learn	Net worth; alternatives; term life insurance; 529s, if applicable
Enjoy	Potential early retirement; college graduations, if applicable; paying off your mortgage

Walk You To WEALTH

We are now in the phase of moderate impact money babies. You may be at your peak from an earnings perspective, but time is slowly moving against you, and you may only have 15 years of money babies if we assume retirement at age 65. Again, you shouldn't be discouraged as it's never too late to start. It just means that you need to work that much harder to invest more during this period of peak earnings. Hopefully you also have a lot to celebrate, including potential college graduations, paying off your home, or maybe even an early retirement. You should also start determining how to build cash reserves for retirement, hopefully 2-3 years' worth as opposed to the 3-6 months during working years.

Age: 60s	
Save	Amount: 2-3 years of essential expenses Account: Online bank Debt: Eliminate and/or avoid credit card debt; pay down mortgage
Invest	Amount: 10%-30% of gross salary Accounts: By prioritization & automated Allocation: 90% boring, 10% fun
Money Babies	Low impact
Patience	Delayed gratification; avoid lifestyle inflation
Learn	Net worth; alternatives; term life insurance; 529s, if applicable
Enjoy	Retirement; being mortgage free; wealth (having choice)

Walk You To WEALTH

We are now in a phase of low impact money babies, but with some planning, you should be approaching your destination on our walk to wealth. This is hopefully a time of enjoyment, giving back, and little worry about money. If you've reached financial independence, this is all about "choice," and deciding how you want to spend your time. As Henry David Thoreau said, "Wealth is the ability to fully experience life," and if you've sacrificed some of that life to reach a comfortable retirement in your 60s, then you should certainly enjoy all the experiences you deserve. One critical factor to being able to enjoy this money you've worked so hard to accumulate is completely outside of your control but may have a tremendous impact on your future. It's known by yet another complicated financial term, sequence of returns risk. I call it Connect4 risk. Hopefully, you are familiar with the classic board game Connect4. If you aren't, it's a game where each player takes turns sliding discs into a space on the board and the objective is to connect four discs horizontally, vertically, or diagonally to win. I play a fair amount with my kids and sometimes my wife, but she wins too often for me to find it very enjoyable. We ordinarily flip a coin to see who goes first, which in our house isn't a real coin, but rather asking our Google smart speaker to flip a coin. This is the Connect4 risk. Connect4 allows the first player to win every time, regardless of their opponent's moves, if played perfectly. In other words, there is a distinct advantage and disadvantage to the order of game play which in my case is randomly decided by my smart speaker. Imagine automatically losing a game because of a random coin flip. This Connect4 risk of going second is essentially a sequence of returns risk. You are at a disadvantage by factors that are outside of your control, and you will ultimately lose the game, only this isn't a child's game, but rather your ability to make your money last in retirement. Let's go a bit deeper and see how this applies to your investments.

From an investment perspective, Connect4 risk means that if you are starting to withdraw from your portfolio during a period of time which coincides with a down market or recession, it will have a significant impact on your ability to make your money last through a typical 30-year retirement. In other words, if after you retire the market averages 0% or a negative return for your first 5 or 10 years, which is entirely possible, this has devastating effects when compounded by your need to withdraw money during these early retirement years. As I mentioned, this is outside of your control, but will likely result in you losing this very critical financial game. For a quick visualization, imagine if your checking account was simultaneously being used to pay bills and also slowly and magically dwindling. Much like how our money babies compound over time, this has the counter effect during down or bear markets and due to the fact that market swings and cycles are unpredictable and uncontrollable, there are limited ways to mitigate it; however, below are a few strategies in preferential order:

1. Work longer - This may not be optimal or even possible for you, but it's one way to counter Connect4 risk. Perhaps a middle ground is a side-hustle or working part-time in a similar field that you just retired from. There have also been multiple studies on the positive mental effects of working longer, especially if you can leave a potentially soul sucking job for something you enjoy.

2. Build multiple income streams - If you have multiple income streams, this will help offset the impact of a lower stock or bond market. For example, if you have rental income or are earning interest from staking

cryptocurrency, these may help to offset the amount you need from your traditional investments.

3. Reduce spending - You can simply cut back on your spending during these early years, but again, this will be less than optimal as you want to enjoy these years as much as possible.

4. Diversify - We discussed asset allocation at length earlier, including the typical inverse relationship between the U.S. and international stock markets. The ability to diversify may allow you to offset some of this risk.

5. Use cash reserves - Although the value of your cash is eroded by inflation, I would build substantial cash reserves for retirement, approximately 2-3 years' worth depending on your number of income streams. Ideally, this money would be for life's unexpected expenses during a period of time where you aren't actively earning income, but it can also be used in your early retirement to stave off Connect4 risk.

6. Social security - I don't like the idea of taking social security early for those in the U.S. because you can receive approximately 132% more by delaying until age 70; however, you can always claim early, if needed.

7. Get lucky - This clearly isn't a strategy, but you could get lucky! Over the course of a 30-year retirement, you will go through multiple market cycles; however, it's in these first few years of retirement where the damage could be severe. I'd rather not leave it up to luck, but it's an option!

Chapter Eight: Final Thoughts

"Sometimes the questions are complicated and the answers are SIMPLE."

Dr. Seuss

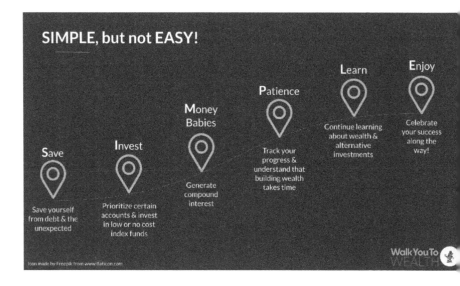

I hope you enjoyed our walk and feel better about your path towards wealth. If there is a final sentiment to leave you with, it's that this is SIMPLE, but not easy. The key is to start. As I mentioned too many times before, starting yesterday would have been better than today, but starting today is infinitely better than waiting until tomorrow. There will be bumps in the road, detours, and missteps along the way, but there will also be huge wins, celebrations, and a tremendous sense of satisfaction during your walk to wealth.

In an ideal world, you know more now than you did before picking up this book and also can revisit chapters or sections as you cross different parts of the walk. In today's world, the word wealth is oftentimes associated with negative connotations as we discuss problems, such as the wealth gap, but I view wealth and financial education as the solution, not the problem. It truly is the ability to fully experience life and I'm not sure why anyone wouldn't want a roadmap to that destination!

Lastly, I want to continue this conversation and am available via Twitter (@walkyoutowealth) or my site www.WalkYouToWealth.com. I'd love to hear about your journey and what sections of this book resonated with you or could have been better. Much like our walk together, this book wasn't about perfection, but rather providing you with SIMPLE steps and a partner on your long walk to wealth!

ABOUT THE AUTHOR

Kevin C. Feig wants you to be wealthy!

He grew up in Queens N.Y. and attended Fairfield University, where he earned a Bachelor of Science in Accounting and a Master's in Business Administration. He has spent approximately 20 years working in traditional financial services and the cryptoeconomy.

He is also a CERTIFIED FINANCIAL PLANNER™, a Certified Public Accountant, and a Personal Financial Specialist, but most importantly he's created an honest, authentic, and simple approach to personal finance in his first book, *Walk You to Wealth*. He lives with his amazing wife and two incredible kids in Massachusetts.

For more information visit WalkYouToWealth.com.

REFERENCES

[i] Killingsworth, M. A. (2021). Experienced well-being rises with income, even above $75,000 per year. *Proceedings of the National Academy of Sciences, 118*(4). https://doi.org/10.1073/pnas.2016976118

[ii] Arnold, J., & Images, G. (2012, July 6). *The stuff of families*. The Wall Street Journal. Retrieved from https://www.wsj.com/articles/SB1000142405270230 4708604577504672437027392

[iii] *How to plan for Rising Health Care Costs*. Fidelity. (2022, May 25). Retrieved from https://www.fidelity.com/viewpoints/personal-finance/plan-for-rising-health-care-costs

[iv] *Asset allocation: Key to your investment Climate*. Vanguard. (n.d.). Retrieved from https://investor.vanguard.com/investor-resources-education/how-to-invest/asset-allocation

[v] Gallo, J. J., & Chen, H. (2011, April 1). *Portfolio success rates: Where to draw the line*. Financial Planning

Association. Retrieved from https://www.financialplanningassociation.org/article/journal/APR11-portfolio-success-rates-where-draw-line

[vi] *DALBAR's 22nd Annual Quantitative Analysis of Investor Behavior* (2015) *Hubspot.net.* Available at: https://cdn2.hubspot.net/hubfs/5341408/EP_Wealth_Advisors_April2019/pdf/2016-Dalbar-QAIB-Report.pdf

[vii] Stevens, P. (2021, March 24). *This chart shows why investors should never try to time the stock market.* CNBC. Retrieved from https://www.cnbc.com/2021/03/24/this-chart-shows-why-investors-should-never-try-to-time-the-stock-market.html

[viii] Arnott, A. C. (2019, November 14). *Revisiting the case for International.* Morningstar, Inc. Retrieved from https://www.morningstar.com/articles/954560/revisiting-the-case-for-international

Printed in the USA
CPSIA information can be obtained
at www.ICGtesting.com
LVHW061950120923
757983LV00010B/371

9 781088 093382